Donald Trump

Inside Trump's Indictment and Legal Battle

(The Superseding Indictment of Donald Trump With New Charges)

Bernard Smith

Published By **Jordan Levy**

Bernard Smith

All Rights Reserved

Donald Trump: Inside Trump's Indictment and Legal Battle (The Superseding Indictment of Donald Trump With New Charges)

ISBN 978-1-7774561-5-3

No part of this guidebook shall be reproduced in any form without permission in writing from the publisher except in the case of brief quotations embodied in critical articles or reviews.

Legal & Disclaimer

The information contained in this book is not designed to replace or take the place of any form of medicine or professional medical advice. The information in this book has been provided for educational & entertainment purposes only.

The information contained in this book has been compiled from sources deemed reliable, and it is accurate to the best of the Author's knowledge; however, the Author cannot guarantee its accuracy and validity and cannot be held liable for any errors or omissions. Changes are periodically made to this book. You must consult your doctor or get professional medical advice before using any of the suggested remedies, techniques, or information in this book.

Upon using the information contained in this book, you agree to hold harmless the Author from and against any damages, costs, and expenses, including any legal fees potentially resulting from the application of any of the information provided by this guide. This disclaimer applies to any damages or injury caused by the use and application, whether directly or indirectly, of any advice or information presented, whether for breach of contract, tort, negligence, personal injury, criminal intent, or under any other cause of action.

You agree to accept all risks of using the information presented inside this book. You need to consult a professional medical practitioner in order to ensure you are both able and healthy enough to participate in this program.

Table Of Contents

Chapter 1: The Rise Of Donald Trump 1

Chapter 2: The Trump Presidency 21

Chapter 3: Trump's Leadership Style And Communication Strategies 43

Chapter 4: The Trump Administration's Legacy 66

Chapter 5: Post-Presidency And Future Influence 89

Chapter 6: Donald Trump A Stem 112

Chapter 7: A Narrow Escape 121

Chapter 8: Trump Stoops To Conquer .. 126

Chapter 9: Business Lessons From Trump-1986 Entrepreneur Of The Year 134

Chapter 10: Every Nation Needs A Good Foundation 151

Chapter 11: Designing Your Blueprint To Success 166

Chapter 12: Wheeling And Dealing Like Donald Trump 175

Chapter 1: The Rise Of Donald Trump

The ascendance to the presidency of Donald Trump in American legislative matters was a rare event that was the subject of worldwide attention. An expert in finance and a non-scripted TV personality, Trump challenged conventional political norms and rose to the highest-profile office on the US. In this piece we'll examine the main factors contributing to Best's rise and the impact it had in American political questions.

Libertarian Allure:

One of the most notable aspects of the presidency was Trump's liberty-minded stance. Trump took advantage of the anger and disappointment that a large portion of the American populace. Trump declared himself to be a rebel who would "clean up the terrible land" within Washington, D.C., as well as fight for the plight of common people. The unfiltered, clear correspondence style echoed the sentiments of many voters that felt disengaged from conventional public representatives.

Disorderly Feeling:

The rise of Trump also reflected the more widespread spirit of resolute excitement that was sweeping across the US. A lot of Americans found themselves confused by the foundation of their political system and long to see a changes. Trump was untouchable, and with his status, promised to shake into the system and shake the boat. The attraction was particularly compelling to those in the Rust Belt, which is which Trump's remarks on the exchange of goods and assurances for employment resonated through networks that were ravaged due to the decline of the monetary system.

Media and Marking:

Trump's time as a scripted TV character gave his a distinct advantage when it came to being able to attract media attention. Trump was a master of media control and utilised online entertainment venues such as Twitter to talk openly with his friends, avoiding traditional media outlets. His shrewd assertions and arousing manner of speaking led to massive media coverage and further fulfilled his purpose and increased the extent of his reach.

Movement and Patriotism:

Trump's extremely hardline approach to migration has resonated with a large portion of the American population who are concerned about security at the border and personal. Trump's pledge to build an unidirectional wall across that U.S.- Mexico boundary and calls for tighter immigration policies resonated with those who believe the notion that American concerns should be the first to figure the process. Trump's patriotism resonated with voters that felt shackled by the globalization process and rapid segment change.

Unhappy with social sensitivity

Trump's capacity to speak his thoughts in a candid manner without sticking to a semblance of sensitivity was just another point of view that resonated with many of his supporters. Trump's brash and sometimes controversial remarks earned him the reputation as an uncompromising person, and his supporters appreciated the unfiltered manner in which he spoke. In an time when political discourse has become more and more shrewd his candor appealed to people who felt that their concerns were not being taken seriously or silenced.

The rise of Donald Trump was a mind amazing and complicated political phenomenon. The appeal of his egalitarian nature, the indefatigable feeling, the dominance of the media, his marking the position of movement and a skepticism of any overt sensitivities have all contributed to his success. However one may feel of Trump His administration, it was able to make a significant change in American legislation and touched off debates about issues such as patriotic patriotism and populism as well as the role of traditional institutions of political power. Recognizing the forces that pushed Trump to lead is essential to understand the changing landscape of the current political landscape.

1.1 Early Life And Background

Donald John Trump, brought to the world on the 14th of June 1946 within Sovereigns, New York City He is a famous

American financial manager, television persona, and official in the US government. Trump is known because he was the 45th President of the US between January 20th 2017 until January 20, 2021.

Donald Trump was the fourth of five children brought to the world by Frederick C. also, Mary MacLeod Trump. His father was a great land engineer and his mother was the typical Scottish outcast. As a child, Trump went to the Kew-Woods School in Sovereigns however afterward, he attended the New York Military Foundation, which he was able to excel both academically and physically.

After moving away from the secondary school system in the year 1964, Trump attended Fordham College for a considerable amount of time before moving on towards Wharton College. Wharton School of the College of Pennsylvania. Trump graduated from

Wharton in 1968 and earned the degree of a financial analyst. While in school, Trump was profoundly impacted by the land enterprise of his father and gained a significant amount of experiences working with his father's business during his summer vacations.

After his graduation, Trump became a partner in his dad's company known as the Trump Association that focused on land development within New York City. The company immediately began engaging in various large-scale projects such as his involvement in the development of private structures such as hotels, inns, and clubs. In the 70s, Trump was well-known as a land developer and gained respect for his arduous undertakings as well as his extravagant way of living.

Through his career, Donald Trump became inseparable from excess and luxury He frequently ties himself to major events and famous people. In spite of his travels Trump also branched out into other activities, including diversion and even facilitating the unscripted TV show "The Understudy" that aired between 2004 and the year 2015.

Trump's involvement in legislative matters began in the latter half of the 80s. He declared his interest in public initiatives and frequently spoke about policies-related questions. It was not until 2015 that Trump announced his candidacy to the presidency of the US. He was portrayed as a rising conservative, Trump acquired consideration with controversial remarks, his the libertarian way of talking and promises to "Make America Incredible Once more."

After winning the Republican nomination, Trump proceeded to overcome the Vote candidate based on her vote, Hillary Clinton, in the presidential election of

2016 and was elected president. The time he served as president was marked by numerous major strategy shifts, such as the change in charge, the liberation effort as well as movement restrictions and exchange conversations. However, his presidency was also marked due to debate and conflict as well as his erratic approach to correspondence and adversity that often required assistance as well as analyses.

Overall the life of Donald Trump's predecessor was defined by his upbringing of a wealthy family and his eagerness to engage in industry of land. Trump benefited from his wealth as a basis for his own personal world and then delved into the realm of legislative matters and eventually turning into the 45th leader in the US.

1.2 Business Ventures And Branding

Donald Trump, the 45th President of the US has a lengthy track record of completing and defining initiatives. Although his political career has received a lot of attention, the recognition of his achievements and impact as a finance executive and business strategist prior to entering the political arena is important.

Trump's responsibilities span many businesses, such as amusement, land, and the concept of cordiality. Trump began his career as a land developer, and continued following the steps of his father, Fred Trump. Trump Properties, the land improvement company founded through Donald Trump, assumed a significant role in shaping and shaping the New York City horizon. The most notable activities include Trump Pinnacle located in Manhattan, Trump Court, as well as Trump World Pinnacle.

The past land Trump expanded his brand into diverse regions. He walked into media organizations through facilitating and hosting the television program that was not scripted "The Student" along with its companion projects that ran over 14 seasons. The openness of TV allowed him to connect with a much larger audience and strengthen his reputation as a skilled financial administrator.

One of the key aspects of the work Donald Trump has undertaken is his mark-making method. Trump has worked hard to create his unique image, which revolves in the direction of extravagant success, lavishness, and achievement. The properties he owns often carry the Trump identity in a clear and distinct manner, while demonstrating the sense of prestige and class. The mark-making efforts of Trump extend beyond the boundaries of land. He has given his approval to numerous items like clothes, perfumes as well as steaks.

But, his projects haven't come without controversy. Although he has had huge successes like the redesign of Wollman Arena in Focal Park and the completion of it early and within the budget however, there were instances of notable business failures too. The most prominent of these are one of them being the Trump Taj Mahal club in Atlantic City, which sought protection from financial risk in the year 1991.

The decisions and actions of President Trump will have an impact on his public image as well as his public recognition. His brand and name have become synonymous with wealth and excess, which drew his two ally and critics alike. It was a key aspect in his politic goals which culminated in his enlightening campaign in the year 2016.

Overall, Trump's actions and efforts have created a crucial impact on the various enterprises. Land improvements, diversion experiences, and the cautious development of his personal image have formed his image in the eyes of the world and have played an essential role in his professional life. Although his successes and failures are widely discussed, there's no stopping his enduring impact from gaining his name and the recognition it demands.

1.3 Involvement in Politics The Apprenticeship and the Status of Celebrity

Trump's experience in the legislative arena was heavily influenced through his successful TV career particularly his role as host of the live, unscripted series "The Student" as well as his renowned position. Even though it was true that he'd played around with the legislative process prior to "The Understudy" the show that truly brought his name into the limelight and laid the foundation for his potential official role.

"The Student" premiered in 2004, the show's structure revolved around a room full of potential candidates seeking a position within The Trump Association. The program quickly turned into an instant hit with Trump's simple initiative style as well as his business acumen and the expression "You're exiled!" As host and leadership creator, Trump turned into an instantly recognized brand, and the charismatic Trump captivated audiences.

With "The Understudy," Trump established a reputation as an efficient, unambiguous, and a savvy financial expert. In the show, he was portrayed as a professional in bargain-making and someone who was able to turn bombing businesses around. This portrayal was echoed by many viewers who were impressed by Trump's success and wealth.

Benefiting from his newly recognized his status as a VIP, Trump decisively situated himself before the world's eyes. He appeared on news and other syndicated projects and even, quite unexpectedly, he branched out into various forms of media such as publications and products. Trump's name was a synonym for his accomplishments and plushness, making his image an unmistakable persona.

The mixture of Trump's TV appearance, his big name fame as well as his business fame provided the foundation for his eventual announcement on legislative issues. In 2015, Trump reported his administration's office and at first raised eyes among observers of politics and experts. But his praise and the capacity to command media considerations pushed the agenda forward as his use of virtual entertainment was a major factor and he organized massive scale rallies in order to connect with his supporters.

Trump's rise to power demonstrated the effect of his huge image on the campaign trail. Trump exhibited a rash and jolly style, often having to rely on unsubstantiated statements for his the world. This style of speaking sparked critiques of media coverage and brought on allies who appreciated his determination to question the political base.

Although "The Student" and his infamous position certainly played a significant role in his involvement with governmental matters, it's important to remember the fact that his political ambitions did not solely result of his TV vocation. Trump expressed interest in legislation as early in the 80s, and considered possible presidential runs prior to. Whatever the case the reality of his perception and recognition as a television persona that gave him the stage on which to conclude an effective official campaign.

In a nutshell the way that Donald Trump's entry to the political arena was incredibly affected by his role as presenter for "The Student" as well as his status as a VIP. The program pushed him into the spotlight and established the image of a solid and professional financial advisor. By leveraging his uniqueness, Trump had the option to interact with the electorate and efficiently conclude his official task, eventually becoming the 45th President in the US.

1.4 Presidential Ambitions: Trump's First Candidacy

Donald Trump's most famous bid for the presidency of the US was a pivotal moment in American historical politics.

Trump was a distinct television and land-designer announced his candidacy to run for president on the 16th of June in 2015 during a debate in the Trump Pinnacle located in New York City.

The time came when Trump's candidacy shocked a huge majority. Despite the fact that he'd been an important figure for a considerable time mostly famous for his projects and the show that was unscripted on television "The Understudy" few people anticipated that he would pursue the same career path in politics as well as campaign to be the highest-ranking politician within the nation.

Trump's agenda was a bit out of the ordinary and drew wide-ranging scrutiny throughout. He positioned himself in the role of a villain and vowed to shake up the foundation of politics and shine a spotlight on topics like trade, movement, and the resurgence of money. His sloppy and sometimes disputed style of speech resonated in a segment of the American population who were dissatisfied with the traditional legislative bodies.

In the Republican primaries, Trump went head to head with a handful of well-prepared legislators before emerging as the chief. Trump's pretentious manner, ability to overpower media coverage and his savvy use of internet-based media played a large part in his success. The Trump rally attracted huge audiences, and his message was heard by a large number of Americans feeling abandoned by the globalization process and the advancing economic system.

Despite facing a lot of opposition within his own group, Trump got the conservative choice during the Conservative Public Show in July 2016. Then he went on to challenge Vote selected based Hillary Clinton in the overall election.

The presidential campaign of 2016 was extremely hostile and marked by intense debates as well as a myriad of disputes. Trump's bizarre mission style and aggressive approach to legislative issues attracted both eager allies and passionate commentators. In the end, with a stunning conclusion, Trump tied down an enough number of his supporters for the presidency, beating Clinton on the 8th of November the 8th of November in 2016.

Trump's victory with the political choice of 2016 marked a pivotal moment in American political questions. Trump's administration was described as having an unpredictability and erratic policy style that was often in conflict with standards of the political establishment and testing the laid-out organizations.

Chapter 2: The Trump Presidency

Donald Trump, the 45th President of the US who was elected between January 20th 2017 until January 20 20, 2021. His presidency was the subject in the midst of debate and division across the country and around the world. Below is a summary of the most important aspects that are part of Trump's administration: Trump administration:

Monetary Strategies Monetary Strategies: One important pillar of the Trump administration's goals was his promise to strengthen the American economy. The Trump administration implemented taxes, liberalization measures as well as sought trade strategies that were protectionist, recollecting the need to impose duties on different goods. Allies argue that these agreements led to the financial development and low unemployment rates and record-breaking securities exchange prices. However, some experts argue they are adamant that the benefits foreseeably favor to the wealthy, and the long-term effects of these strategies remain a mystery.

Line Strategies and Movement Trump's stance on immigration was deeply questioned. He backed tighter line controls, which included the development of an American-Mexico border wall line. The group he was associated with implemented an approach known as the "Zero Resilience" strategy, which led to the separation of families on the line and drew extensive conclusions. This strategy was later changed after public outrage. Trump also attempted to implement movement bans against certain transcendentally Muslim nations that faced actual challenges.

International strategy Strategy for international relations: International strategy: Trump group sought the "America first" approach to international issues, focusing on securing American interests while focusing on bilateral exchanges. Trump has withdrawn the US from peace agreements such as those referred to as the Paris Environment Accord and the Iran Atomic Arrangement, attesting that they did not serve American interest. Trump also participated in high-risk discussions between North Korea, meeting with Kim Jong-un, its leader in order to tackle the nuclear threat in Korea's Korean Promontory.

Relations with the media: Through his entire presidency, Trump much of the time was at odds with the media. He often characterized their publication as "counterfeit information." Trump embraced virtual entertainment, specifically Twitter to provide an instant way to engage with people in general of the country, often bypassing traditional media sources. His relationships with the media was not a good one some pundits asserting his actions ruined the press and cultivated a climate where columnists were viewed as antagonists.

Affair: Donald Trump turned into the third president in US history to face a rebuke in the Place of Delegates. The principal arraignment, which took place in December 2019, held him accountable for a lack of respect for force and obstruction of Congress related to his interactions with Ukraine. The Senate was cleared at the end of February in 2020. In January 2021, charged the senator of "prompting the rebellion" after the violent riots that erupted in the US Legislative centre with a group of his supporters. The Senate hearing took place just after his resignation which led to his dissolution over and over.

It's crucial to pay attention to that widely-reported assessment of Trump's presidency. It is awe-inspiring. Allies applaud his efforts to reenergize the political base, concentrate on the American economy, and call to change the way that immigrants travel. Experts, on the other hand criticize his erratic way of speaking, his questionable arrangement as well as his handling of diverse issues both domestically and internationally. The Trump administration is always the subject of intense debate and scrutiny.

2.1 The 2016 Presidential Campaign

Donald Trump's 2016 official Mission was an enormous and unpredictable political event that had an impact on American legislation. As the conservative alliance's newcomer, Donald J. Trump was a manager of money and an TV star who was not scripted, took off on the 16th of June in 2015 and went on to win the nomination of his party. The following are some of the key aspects of his job:

Equalitarian Stage: The Trump campaign was based on a liberal stage, which resonated with many Americans unhappy by the foundation of their political system. Trump focused on areas such as exchange, movement and public security, promising the nation to "Make America Extraordinary Once more."

Signature Trademarks: Trump's campaign included key slogans such as "Make America Incredible Once more" and "America First." The slogans enthused those who sought an improvement and more confident approach to protecting American rights.

A dubious migration position A key features of Trump's campaign was that there were major points of strength to him in regards to movement. He demanded development of an unifying wall across that U.S.- Mexico line and claimed that it will enhance public security and combat illicit movements.

The Correspondence and Media Technique
In the course of his mission, Trump utilized internet-based entertainment, specifically Twitter for its ability to effortlessly attract his supporters and bypass traditional media outlets. The tweets he posted, which were unfiltered and provocative, often stood out as important and drew huge attention.

The most important triumphs of Trump's presidency: His mission was a challenge to rivals within his Conservative Alliance during the essential choices. In spite of that, he achieved surprising gains, including winning crucial states, and eventually gaining the nomination of his party.

The gimmicks and the style of speech: Trump's role was distinguished due to his unique style and his manner of speaking. Trump often used contradictory words as well as personal assaults on enemies that resulted in both fierce assistance areas to and against.

Rust Belt Allure: Trump focused his attention on people living in Rust Belt states, who have experienced financial declines and a number of employment problems. The promises he made to bring back blue collar jobs resonated for a lot of the average voters who reside who reside in these states.

The results of the 2016 election are disturbing. Even though he was atop the polls, Donald Trump won the 2016 presidential race with the majority of the appointive vote, but losing the well-known votes for Hillary Clinton. The victory was seen as an extreme steamed, and demonstrated the divide between urban and rural America.

This year's Official Mission was notable in its colossal nature and the discussions surrounding Trump's candidacy. The event marked a shift in American legislation and prepared for the upcoming changes in the political landscape as well as discussions across the country.

2.2 Policy Initiatives and Controversial Decisions

Donald Trump, the 45th leader of the US has had a range of approaches decisions and a few questionable ones during his tenure as President. Below are some of his key characteristics:

Tax reductions and the Occupations Act one of the most important strategies of the Trump group included the Tax breaks and Occupations Act that was passed in 2017. This law would reduce the cost of personal and corporate expenses and also work to improve duty codes, as well as animate financial development. Allies believed that it brought an opportunity to both family members of the working class, whereas experts argued that it primarily helped the wealthiest and increase the burden on public debt.

The Liberation Plan: Trump sought after a strong liberation program, which would mean to reduce unofficial laws across diverse ventures, specifically with regard to nature-based assurances, cash and medical care. The supporters of the plan argued that it will encourage financial development and reduce the burden on businesses, whereas opponents expressed concerns about the likely negative impacts on wellbeing and climate.

Moving Strategies: Trump carried out a couple of questionable immigration arrangements that were generally well-known, including an eminently "Zero Resilience" approach that led to the division of children who are traveling with their family members on the U.S.- Mexico line. This policy was met with a wide-ranging research on its compassion implications and triggered open opposition and legal challenges.

Travel Boycott: In the year 2017, Trump gave Leader Request 13769, often referred to as a "travel boycott." The basic reinterpretation of the request was to halt entry to the US for residents from seven heavily Muslim countries. The boycott movement faced legal issues and had to undergo changes, resulting in different emphasises. Some experts argued that the movement had unjustly identified people based on their religious or ethnic background, however, allies maintained the necessity of it for security reasons.

Paris Arrangement as well as Environmental Change: The Trump group announced the United States' withdrawal of the Paris Understanding which was a global accord that aimed to combat the effects of climate change. The move was met with criticism from naturalists as well as global pioneers who claimed it undermined global efforts in addressing the issue of environmental emergency.

Options for Exchange: Trump sought after a protectionism approach to exchanges, ensuring that taxes are not evaded and reviewing economic agreements such as those of the North American International alliance (NAFTA) that was replaced with the US Mexico-Canada Understanding (USMCA). Many experts have expressed concern about adverse effects on global exchange as well as the possibility of fights over exchanges. However, supporters claimed that the actions were intended to secure American companies and their positions.

Strategy for international relations: Trump's foreign strategies included the relocation to Jerusalem of the U.S. consulate in Israel to Jerusalem as well as the negotiation of the Iran nuclear agreement, as well as the start of negotiations between the U.S. and North Korea over its atomic weapon program. The actions were received by a mix of assistance and analysis. Those who opposed the move who advocated a more resolute U.S. position and pundits warning of the potential consequences for strategic reasons.

It's important to be aware of the fact the fact that opinions on the arrangement drive and decisions vary widely and this summary doesn't capture the entirety of Trump's presidency.

2.3 Foreign Relations: Diplomacy and Global Impact

Trump's foreign relations, as well as his global impact during his presidency were explained by a unique method of dealing with discretionary decisions that often diverged off from normative standards. This is a brief description of his unpredictability in relationship, his strategy and the global impact:

America First Strategy: Donald Trump's "America First" strategy was the central element in his new policy of relations. Trump was focused on protecting American concerns and reconsidering peaceful agreements in order to secure his ideal result to the US.

The Exchange Relationship: Trump planned to reshape international exchange relations. He claimed that the present structure was detrimental to the US.

Trump decided to withdraw of the Transoceanic Organization (TPP) and began a process of renegotiation for the North American International alliance (NAFTA) and introducing the United States Mexico-Canada Understanding (USMCA).

China: Trump took an aggressive stance on China by claiming it was an important contender while blaming China for rogue exchange practices. His group imposed levies against Chinese items and was involved in a trade war that caused serious financial pressures on the two largest economies.

North Korea: Trump sought for a different way to handle North Korea by taking part directly in the discretion of Kim Jong-un, the head of North Korea. The result was a memorable high point between the two leaders but progress with the denuclearization process was halted.

Center East: The Trump administration has announced a number of critical changes in U.S. strategy in the Center East. Incredibly, they saw Jerusalem as being the capital city of Israel and shifted to establish the U.S. to an international safe zone to there. They also expedited their implementation of the Abraham Accords, normalizing strategic relationships between Israel as well as a handful of nations in the Middle East.

Iran Atomic Arrangement Trump has withdrawn from the US of the Iran nuclear agreement, which is officially called the Joint Complete Game plan (JCPOA). Trump claimed that the agreement was not a good one and demanded a most strenuous crusade against Iran with expanded sanctions.

NATO as well as European Partners: Trump every time he spoke, he condemns NATO people in his view of lack of financial engagement in the collusion. Trump demanded a broader protection budget from European allies and voiced doubt on the merits in multilateral foundations.

Worldwide Environment Understanding: Trump declared the US's abandonment of the Paris Arrangement, a worldwide effort to combat environmental degradation. The decision prompted a huge amount of international scrutiny, with a variety of nations affirming their commitment to the agreement.

Global Discernment and Impact Trump's erratic approach to approach strategy and his shrewd nature often led to conflict and mixed responses across the globe. Trump's administration triggered debate regarding the future of American power and its global need for it, leading to adjustments in global factors and strategic links.

It is crucial to be aware of the fact that this report provides an overview of the Trump's foreign relations, as well as its global impact. The advice of obtaining additional viewpoints and sources to get a deeper understanding of this enigma is always recommended.

2.4 Impeachment Proceedings and Acquittal The process of denunciation and subsequent resignation from Donald Trump, the 45th President of the US marked a notable 2nd in American political matters. The situation that unfolded over two occasions and had broad implications on the nation's political environment and triggered serious debates across with the rest of the world over. It is important to understand the intricacies of Donald Trump's court proceedings and inevitable confirmation.

First Denunciation: Ukraine Discussion

The main reprimand processes for Donald Trump occurred in late the year 2019 and into mid-2020. The reason for the charge was a dispute over the Trump's connections to Ukraine. There was a claim that he was able to force to force the Ukrainian government to investigate Joe Biden who is likely to be his candidate for 2020's presidential election, through not releasing the military's guidelines. Liberals believed that this act was a misuse of force, and a stifling of Congress.

On December 18, 2019 The Place of Agents, constrained by liberals, decried Trump with allegations of abuse of force and obstruction of Congress. In the next phase, the indictment process from that point on, was transferred into the Senate in which the preliminary hearing was held. On 5 February 2020 the Senate put out a vote in order to discharge Donald Trump on the two accusations. The Senate decision was largely based on party lines and conservatives gaining majority in the vote and casting a vote in favor of vindication, whereas liberals overwhelmingly voted in favor of their conviction.

Second Arrest: State House Revolt

The second trial process for Donald Trump unfurled in mid 2021 following the events on January 6. That day the 6th of January, a ferocious gathering of Trump allies attacked at the U.S. State house, which resulted in numerous fatalities as well as injuries and destruction to the building. A number of officials and others believed Trump responsible for triggering the uprising by his statements and actions prior to the event.

On the 13th of January in 2021 The Place of Agents, indeed controlled by liberals charged Trump for the instigation of an insurgency. The article describing the arraignment stated the fact that Trump was the one who "seriously threatened his security and that of the US and the underlying principles of governance." The Senate trial began at the end of February, 2021. It which in all cases led to the vindication of Trump in the month of February. Seven Conservative lawmakers cast a vote to find guilty, the greater portion was insufficient to satisfy the majority of 66% of those expected to get conviction.

Political and Legitimate Ramifications:

The process of prosecution and the subsequent exonerations for Donald Trump were profoundly disruptive. The supporters of Trump asserted that the accusations were politically motivated and unsound in their proofs and his opponents argued to argue that his conduct justified a denunciation and conviction.

The absoluteions did not result in any legal violations against Trump aside from conveyed election outcomes. The vindications of Trump have allowed him to run for president once again later in the future, and keep in the air speculation about his planned return to the field of politics.

Reprimands and exonerations mark a significant turning point in American historical political debate. They exposed deep divisions within the United States and spurred debates about the boundaries of the official's power as well as law and order as well as the responsibilities of government officials. While the nation is grappling with the results of these incidents and the impact of President the Trump's trial and subsequent exoneration is likely to continue shaping American public policy for an extended time in the near future.

Chapter 3: Trump's Leadership Style And Communication Strategies

Donald Trump's style of initiative and methods of correspondence were shocking during his tenure as 45th President of the US from 2017 until 2021. The way he conducted himself was most more of the time described as a fascinating combination of certainty, apoplism as well as erratic tactics. Below are some of the most important elements of Trump's strategy of initiative as well as his systems for correspondence:

Libertarian Allure: Trump's administration style was based on populism. He spoke straight to the concerns and desires of his core friends. Trump portrayed himself as an outsider, attempting to test the political agenda he laid out by highlighting his capability to communicate with everyday Americans and pledging to concentrate on their interests.

Direct Correspondence Trump was well-known for his direct and concise manner of correspondence. He often eluded traditional channels, and spoke directly to the general public via online entertainment channels, particularly Twitter. Twitter's tweets are often non-filtered, unbranded and provocative. This allowed his followers to avoid media monitors and communicate his thoughts clearly to his followers.

Fundamental and Vital Information: Trump was talented at making use of simple, memorable words to convey his most important message. His slogans, like, "Make America Incredible Once more" as well as "America First" resonated with supporters and became uplifting tears for his campaign as well as his administration. Trump's letter writing style relied on repetition and highlighting important audio files to strengthen his information.

Profound attraction: Trump frequently spoke to emotions, rather than focusing into only the facts and the subtleties of his strategy. Trump used narratives as well as episodic evidence to entice his audience and create a sense of association. The method allowed the artist to capitalize on fears or disappointment as well as any expectation of his fellows creating a strong connection.

A disputed as well as Polarizing Way of talking: Trump's method of communication frequently featured a an unpopular and controversial way of talking. Trump was well-known for using controversial language, making personal threats, as well as participating in mockery that generated significant media coverage. The way he portrayed himself enthused his supporters however, it also attracted criticism from his adversaries as well as a handful of people from his own political party.

Exclusion of Customary Organizations: Trump often portrayed himself as an agitator for the established order and also criticized the traditional media, political rivals as well as regulation frameworks. He attempted to undermine the organizations he considered as obstacles in his plans and maintained a ferocious stance toward them.

Unusual Correspondence Channels: despite the use of Twitter, Trump depended vigorously on meetings, question and answer discussions, and informal media appearances to talk to people on a general level. He was adamant about direct involvement to allies and often keeping huge scopes alive even following his election.

Individual Notes: Trump was talented at developing and marketing his personal image by leveraging his position as a successful financial expert and a TV show character that was not scripted. Trump often infused his letters by incorporating elements of dramatic ability display, self-advancement, and exhibition and helped in getting attention and retaining important areas of strengths to a film.

It's important to note the fact that Trump's style of administration and his methods for correspondence were extremely problematic, giving both of his allies having areas of weakness in and. The effectiveness and adequacy of his method varied between different sections of the population and was contingent upon the development of discussions and investigation.

3.1 The Art of the Deal: Trump's Negotiation Tactics

The book by Donald Trump "The art of bargaining," gives understanding into his strategies for discussion and negotiation. It is important to keep in mind that the strategies might not be typically effective, they do provide an overview of Trump's method of negotiations. These are the key methods of discussion that appear throughout the text:

Imagine something extraordinary: Trump underlines the significance of delineating aggressive goals as well as thinking beyond the obvious. In imagining the best outcomes, he acknowledges that dealings are based on a sense that is a sense of community.

Influence: Trump stresses the meaning of influence when it comes to any trade. This can include having elective options, one-of-a particular mastery, or significant assets that will give you an advantage. Influence could give you more opportunities for exchange, and increase your chances of getting your ideal results.

Be prepared: Trump frequently embraces an extreme arrangement position in order that he can increase his personal benefits. Trump suggests being assertive and proving your point of view clearly and being able to walk away if necessary. It is expected that this approach will demonstrate strength and sway compromises with the opposition.

Understand your enemy: Recognizing what the opposition party's needs as well as their needs, desires, and weaknesses is crucial. Trump recommends conducting a careful investigation and research to gain insights of the motives and motivations of those that you're negotiating with. This data allows you to modify your strategy and make your argument in a way as to appeal to their preferences.

Be the top in communication: Effective writing is an essential element of good discussions. Trump highlights the importance of writing a compelling and clear correspondence that is focused using simple and clear words, as well as making your arguments sound confident.

Set a goal to get moving: Trump accepts that making an urgent need to move forward could help move discussions forward and pressure the opposing party to agree on concessions. If you include cutoff dates and expected open doors that are not working or a restricted access point to another party to take action faster and even negotiate an optimal agreement.

Connections: Although Trump is well-known for his charismatic style however, he also sees benefits of establishing relationships. Trump suggests settling on a common interest, setting out connections, and creating an environment that is conducive to talks. Establishing trust and fostering an atmosphere of order could lead to more effective discussions and generally beneficial results.

It is crucial to keep in mind that the strategies used to discuss issues can be altered dependent on the particular circumstances, the people involved as well as social considerations. Though a number of these methods may be effective in the case of Trump in certain situations but they might not be generalized or effective for everyone. The ability to adapt and change is essential when using exchange strategies.

3.2 The Trump Persona: Brashness and Boldness

Trump's personality can be seen through his irresponsibility and power. In all his life, Trump has gained notoriety as a person who is honest, confident and playful with his methods. His recklessness as well as determination has been the hallmark of his career in politics and general public profile.

Unpredictability is a key aspect of the Trump persona. Trump is well-known for his candid and often boring correspondence style that could appear to be a bit controversial or even threatening to others. Trump does not shy away from giving his opinions regardless of whether they're deemed to be politically absurd or untrue. Trump's recklessness is evident when he engages in online entertainment venues such as Twitter and Instagram, where he will often engage in direct and non-filtered conversations with his followers as well as pundits in the same. The unrestrained manner has impressed his supporters and prompted analysis from those who oppose him.

Trump's strengths are a second major characteristic. He's never resisted to confront challenges, or even create chaos. In his initiatives to policy-making, Trump has shown a willingness to go against conventional norms, and to pursue his goals with determination. Trump's strength can be seen with his commitments to such things as the construction of walls along the border between Mexico and the United States line or revising the alliance between economics. Even though these pledges were viewed by some with suspicion people, they were echoed by many of his supporters who believed the president to be a refreshing alternative in comparison to the traditional legislators.

Trump's unpredictability and power are is evident in his style of leadership. As the 45th President of the US Trump displayed the desire to shake the established norms and challenge the way we manage the government. The "America First" strategy and unreserved desire to implement strategies in line to his ideals led to him being a controversial figure. His bold choices, like including the pulling away from peaceful agreements such as that of Paris Environment Accord or the Iran Atomic Agreement and being praised by some as an act of unity, whereas others considered them reckless.

It's crucial to be aware of his recklessness and insanity have attracted in a devoted following as well as pulled him on the 'big picture. Allies admire his candor and his willingness to share his thoughts in a candid manner, as well as his evident strength when it comes to defending the things he believes in. But, critics say that his recklessness is destructive, while his strength may be seen as unwise or lacking the nuances.

In general, Trump's personality is distinguished because of his stubbornness and strength. These traits have contributed to his public image along with his political ambitions as well as his administration style. Although some praise his openness and constant pursuit of the goals he has set, other people see his approach as controversial and risky. Whatever the case, there can be no doubt that the president's insanity and power will continue to impact the political landscape.

3.3 Utilizing Social Media: Twitter and the Trump Presidency

The way that Donald Trump used online entertainment, particularly Twitter in his presidency was awe-inspiring and profoundly had an impact on the political arena and the public debate. Trump saw the power of online entertainment platforms to be a quick channel of communication with his friends and also embraced Twitter as a crucial tool to share his views as well as making declarations of strategy and gaining support from all people.

One of the most striking aspects of his Twitter usage was his unfiltered, often controversial manner of speaking. His voice was unmistakably that was accompanied by brief, provocative tweets which evaded the usual guards of the media and allowed the public to speak freely with an array of followers. The tweets he posted were a majority often time packed with personal insults that verbally abused, or inaccurate statements, and earned him applause from his supporters for the authenticity and criticism and criticism from those who opposed him due to his inability to follow protocol.

With his Twitter account with the handle @realDonaldTrump Trump was able to immediately request consideration of media. The tweets he posted became headline news that sparked discussions, debates, and sometimes even approaches that were changed. The stage was used to announce significant decisions such as the demise of officials or the introduction of new strategies, which often surprised himself and his guides. This method of irregularity had dual advantages and disadvantages since it allowed him to keep the account in check, however it also led to irregularities and sometimes confusion within the organization.

His use of the internet for entertainment wasn't limited to only one-way communication; he also efficiently connected to his followers and other pundits. Trump used Twitter as a tool for strengthening his base and sharing his mottos for the campaign, and battling his opponents. Trump's capability to train for his supporters online was apparent when he was on his official trip in 2016 in which his social media presence played a crucial role in helping his base of citizens as well as establishing a strong online-based community. The entire time he was president was in constant contact with his association with his followers and frequently used Twitter to act as a symphony for assessing general opinion as well as gain feedback.

On the other hand, Trump's online entertainment activities weren't without controversy. His tweets were a majority often time condemned for spreading falsehoods and spreading falsehoods while his private tweets go after gatherings, people or other individuals. The behavior that he has engaged in causes the suspension of his account or severely targeted. In actual, Twitter hailed and truth is that they have a lot of his tweets. He also explains methods with combat deception, as well as the spreading of false information that was deposited in their base.

The connection between Trump and Twitter proved to be a lot more violent at the end of his presidency. In the wake of the State House revolt that took place on the 6th of January in 2021 Twitter was for all time removed Trump's name in fear of the risk of further prompting of violence. The move sparked an thorough discussion of the role of online entertainment platforms to control political debate as well as the connection between the possibility for articulation as well as the repercussions of snark.

In summary, Donald Trump's access to virtual entertainment, specifically Twitter during his presidency, profoundly affected the flow of political communication. Trump's unfiltered and provocative manner attracted a wide range of attention which allowed him to effortlessly create the narrative, rally his allies and dictate the way media reports are reported. However, it also sparked debates and raised concerns regarding the spreading of lies and the potential consequences from unrestricted virtual entertainment. Virtual entertainment usage by President Trump could be viewed as a characteristic feature of his administration as well as an issue of ongoing discussion regarding legislation and the media.

3.4 Public Relations and Media Interactions

The media and marketing collaborations were a key element of his career and his presidency. The most well-known for his distinctive way of communicating, Trump utilized different methodologies to connect with the general media and society, often gaining acknowledgement and research. Below are some of the most important concerns regarding the media and advertising collaborations of Best:

Indirect and Unfiltered Correspondence One of the main characteristics that Trump's personal style in correspondence was his desire for clear and unfiltered information. Trump often used online entertainment venues, specifically Twitter for a way to bypass traditional media channels to talk directly with his followers and others all over the world. Twitter's tweets often garnered huge attention and debate, since they are often free of scripts and open.

Unsubstantiated Explanations: Trump's true and sometimes disputed claims were an indication of his advertising strategy. Trump frequently used aggressive language, as well as engaged in fights that were open to the public, including with rivals from the political spectrum and people from the media. Although this strategy influenced his constituency and generated massive media exposure, it also attracted criticism for its disruptive manner.

A regular media commitment: Trump was profoundly apparent throughout his presidency. He regularly held questions and answer sessions. He was often entertaining in heated discussions with columnists. The briefings and meetings he held for the press were renowned for their spirited and zany nature. Trump frequently evaluating writers, as well as giving short, important videos.

Analyzing the traditional press: Trump was straightforwardly reproachful of what he called"the "phony media" media, particularly the standard sources that he believed as a fair representation of him. Trump blamed the media for his tendencies and then repeatedly used the term "counterfeit information" to justify the inequitable inclusion of. His squabbling relations with the media echoed to his allies, yet it also raised concerns over the loss of trust within the media.

Rally-style occasions Rally-style events like Trump's served as an essential device for communicating with his followers and encouraging media participation. The occasions allowed the president to talk with his followers in a straightforward manner, communicate his policies, and empower the people he has embraced. Trump's conferences were frequently deemed in the news because of the size of their groups as well as his intense speeches.

The use of moderate media Trump was a major area where he was a strong candidate for moderate news source, such as Fox News, where he found more considerate acceptance. Trump was consistently in Fox News programs and conceded discussions to moderate hosts using their platform for amplification of the message for an open audience.

Important Uses of Public Interviews: Trump used question and answer sessions with aplomb, occasion, using them to regulate the media's reporting patterns or to evade consideration of combative questions. Question and answer discussions were renowned due to their duration and speed they were frequently used to do an active role in controlling his media coverage and shaping public conversation.

World Media Commitment The Trump administration's collaborations with international media organizations also stood out during the time of his presidency. His interactions with unknown experts and question and answer discussions on the international stage regularly drew massive review and discussion. The collaborations he had with international columnists may differ from his approach to local media, showing the more political inclination.

It's important to pay attention to that general perception of Trump's marketing and media relations changes generally. Allies appreciated his candid manner of speaking and saw it as an attempt to revive traditional political concerns. Some analysts, on the other hand expressed concern over his unorthodox way of speaking, his assault against the media as well as the potential ramifications to the public's confidence and talk within fair organizations.

Chapter 4: The Trump Administration's Legacy

The Trump administration that lasted between Jan. 20, 2017 until the 20th of January in 2021 had a lasting impact on the US as well as the political landscape. Although opinions about his presidency are not always consistent, knowing the most important aspects of the organization's legacy is crucial.

Monetary Strategies Monetary Strategies: One among the most important issues of the Trump administration was the emphasis he placed on economic development as well as the creation of new occupations. The administration implemented charge modifications which included those relating to the Tax breaks and Occupations Demonstration of 2017, which aimed to boost financial growth and reduce corporate duty rates. Allies believe that these agreements helped to boost financial development as well as low unemployment rates prior to the Coronavirus epidemic.

Liberation A.K.A. the Trump group sought Liberation: The Trump organization sought to implement a liberation plan and hoped to reduce government intervention in different aspects in the world economy. It also included reversing the natural rules, financial guidelines and the guidelines that govern the provision of medical services. Allies argue that these changes provided organizations with greater flexibility and opportunities, while also accelerating monetary development. The media, however expressed concerns about the possibility of negative impacts on wellbeing and climate.

International strategy International strategy: The Trump organisation adopted the "America First" way to tackle international strategies that focuses on

American public interest. The Trump organization sought to take an even more unified position on exchanges, and was involved in battles over exchange with other nations, but most significantly China. It also tried to modify economic deals and led to the replacement of NAFTA by the United States Mexico Canada Understanding (USMCA). The group also pursued political initiatives like the infamous Abraham Accords, which standardized relationships between Israel and several nations in the Middle East.

Moving and Boundary Security Boundary Security and Movement Trump group put a massive focus on border and migration security. The organization tried to restrict the movement of people, particularly from countries thought to pose an imminent security threat, via leaders' arrangements and boycotts. It also implemented the "zero resilient" method, which resulted in division of families along that U.S.- Mexico line. The actions earned both praise from those who emphasized the safety of citizens and criticism of those who believed they had violated the common law.

Legal Arrangements: One the longest-running traditions of the Trump group is its influence on the legal executive of the federal government. The president Trump has delegated three Supreme Court judges as well as a variety of federal judges, shaping the basic philosophic balance of the courts for a long time into the into the future. The arrangements were welcomed by those who fought to change the structure of the executive branch as well as pundits expressed concern concerning the expected changes in policy and points of point of reference.

Politics and Polarization Political Talk and Polarization: Trump company was distinguished due to a hypnotic political climate and a hostile discourse. The unpredictable style of correspondence used by President Trump and use of online-based entertainment regularly drew praise as well as criticism. Allies were impressed by his unambiguous character as well as his ability to connect with his supporters, while experts argued that his style of speaking has exacerbated tensions in the United States.

It's crucial to pay attention to that general perception of the Trump group's past is starkly divided. Allies have financial achievements freedom, as well as legal agreements, whereas experts raise concerns in relation to the movement of people, international strategies and its impact of equitable standards. The long and detailed analysis of the Trump Allies' history will likely continue to be the subject of debate and scrutiny for a long time into the future.

4.1 Economic policies and tax Reforms Donald Trump's fiscal strategies and changes to expenses are a key element of his strategy during his presidency. Although it's important to be aware of this information I provide is contingent on the arrangements he has made up the time I reach my insights cutoff September 2021, I will certainly provide you with a description of the key elements of his budget.

Reductions in taxes as well as the Occupations Act (TCJA): The most prominent economic achievements of the Trump group was the passage of that it passed the TCJA on December 31, 2017. The law was intended to make improvements on duty codes and provide relief from charges to individuals and businesses. The key elements of TCJA comprised:

a. Individual tax cuts: The tax law diminished the the annual cost of living for individuals in a couple of sections which provided aid to center salaried workers. The most significant assessed rate for peripherals was lowered down from 39.6 percent to 37 percentage.

b. Reduced corporate assessment rates: The TCJA overall reduced the corporate expenses rate from 35 percentage to 21 percent, plan to improve business performance and attract venture capitalists.

C. Returning home from abroad benefits: The law provided one-time charges on the localized gains from foreign aidiliaries that are part of U.S. organizations, empowering the bringing of benefits for sea travel for the US.

D. Modifications to derivations as well as exclusions: TCJA removed or changed certain allowances and exemptions including reducing the charge for state and neighborhood (SALT) deduction, which covers the interest deduction for home loans as well as expanding the normal allowance.

Liberation: A crucial aspect of Trump's economic agreements was the focus to liberation. The group was designed to ease the burden of administration on businesses in the belief that liberation could spur economic development and job creation. Certain government agencies were tasked with the auditing process and eradicating the existing rules in order to ease the working environment.

Taxes and Exchange: Trump sought after a aggressive exchange program, hoping to secure American enterprises and decrease trade imbalances. Taxes were imposed on imports from a handful of countries, notably China. The goal was to end the issue of unjustifiable exchange practices and encourage homegrown assembly.

a. China exchange war: Trump's group was involved in a dispute over exchange in a dispute with China that enacted taxes on many Chinese goods. The goal was to settle problems, such as safeguarded innovation burglary as well as constrained initiatives to innovate. The exchange war was a major issue with implications for global exchanges as well as caused tensions between two largest economies.

Plans for the framework: Trump upheld for expanded the interest of foundations and even proposed an $1.5 trillion plan to revitalize America's foundation. But, by the time I reached my information cutoff date, this strategy had not yet morphed to be a critical administration activity.

It is essential to be aware of the impact and effectiveness of these approaches are subject of debate among analysts in the market as well as policy makers. Although some argue that tax cuts and freedom stimulate financial development as well as job creation experts are concerned about the impact on distribution of these plans as well as the potential negative impact for the public obligation and whether the exchange duty in achieving their intended purposes.

If you're not in too much problem, keep in mind that budgetary strategies and expense modifications could develop It is recommended to consult further sources and research to gain a thorough understanding about the state of affairs of your ventures.

4.2 Immigration and Border Security

Trump's approach to dealing the issue of line security and immigration was the main focus of his presidency. Throughout his time in office in office, he employed several strategies and stood in the form of explicit steps taken to deal with what he perceived as problems related to the line of control and movement. Important to be aware of the fact that the information provided below is correct to September 2021 as my threshold for understanding will be set at that point.

Line Wall: One of the most memorable aspects of President Trump's travel and border security plans was his pledge to construct a wall separating both the US as well as Mexico. The president claimed that a physical obstruction could deter illegal line crossings, and improve security for the public. As development of this wall was initiated in the administration of President Obama however, it faced a number of challenges such as court fights financial issues, as well as naturally-based concerns. By September 20, 2021 development of the development of the wall was gaining momentum but it was still not yet at the point of completion.

Travel Boycott: Straight out of the gate in his presidency, Trump gave Leader Request 13769. It was later referred to by the name of "travel boycott" or "Muslim boycott." The request was a suspension of entry through the US for those of seven heavily Muslim countries: Iran, Iraq, Libya, Somalia, Sudan, Syria, and Yemen. The boycott of the movement was met with legitimate challenges and was revisited several times. The final version of the boycott that was maintained through the High Court, remembered limitations on entry to and from Iran, Libya, North Korea, Somalia, Syria, Venezuela, and Yemen.

Zero Resistance Strategy: In the year 2018 The Trump organisation implemented an "zero resistance" approach to illegal boundary crossings that led to separation of children with their parents across the border. This policy was the subject of a lot of scrutiny and sparked a protest from the public which led to a subsequent president's request to stop separations between families. But concerns over transients' treatment and conditions of detention facilities were not resolved throughout the Trump administration.

Strategies to Refugees Strategies (Refuge Strategies): The Trump group made some adjustments to the shelter structure. The changes included those of the Transient Security Conventions (MPP) which is also known as"the "Stay In Mexico" strategy. It required specific shelter seekers to remain at Mexico until their cases were dealt with in U.S. movement courts. The organization also sought at limiting shelter eligibility to those who had entered the US illegally, in contrast to those who entered through legitimate ports of entry. The strategies faced legitimate challenges and relied on constant debate.

DACA - The Conceded Activity for the Appearances of Adolescents (DACA) program that was established under the Obama group, offered temporary protection from extradition and work permits to immigrants without documents that arrived in the US when they were young. Under his presidency, Trump looked to end the program but his efforts were thwarted by legal issues. The DACA program remains in operation dependent on proceedings in the courts and on expected official action.

It is crucial to recognize the fact that discussions involving the security of borders and mobility are often a bit confusing and even antagonistic. The opinions on the Trump's strategy and his actions within this realm differ significantly, with certain supporters of his plans to focus on security for the public and enforce the rules of migration, while some opposed the methods and results of his approach, specifically with regard to fundamental questions of freedom and separations between families.

4.3 Environmental and Climate Change Policies

Donald Trump's eco- and climate strategy for change was the topic of debate and controversy throughout his presidency. Some experts suggested that the administration was focused on monetary gains over the natural environment, and his allies appreciated his efforts to push towards what they perceived as challenging policies. Below are some of the most important aspects of Trump's natural and strategy for environmental protection:

Paris Understanding Paris Understanding among the most striking decisions made by the Trump organisation was its decision to withdraw of the Paris Settlement concerning environmental issues. This agreement, which is expected to limit global temperature rise and reduce ozone damaging substances' emission, was accepted by almost every country around the globe. Trump claimed that the agreement was a hindrance to the US economically and did not contribute beneficial to the nation's health.

Clean Power Plan: Trump has coordinated with his Ecological Assessment Organisation (EPA) to examine and ultimately end the Spotless Power Plan, an policy of the Obama administration that aimed to reduce the emissions of fossil fuels that come from power plant. The

EPA acknowledged that the plan placed excessive pressure on coal-related businesses and hindered monetary development.

Reversals on Guidelines In the course of the administration of President Trump was trying to alter different natural rules, arguing that they inhibited economic development and placed unnecessary burdens on businesses. In particular, his administration eased methane emissions by gas and oil actions, repealed the Perfect Water Rule, and affected the rules for vehicle environmental friendliness.

The expansion of non-renewable energy sources: Trump advanced the development of petroleum derivatives made in the United States which includes petroleum, coal and the gas that is flammable. Trump sought to remove boundaries in the pursuit of energy efficiency, for example making more land available to government and oceanward regions to study and development. According to the organization, these steps would boost the autonomy of energy and allow for more occupations.

Ecological Assurance Organization (EPA): Trump delegated Scott Pruitt and was followed by Andrew Wheeler, to lead the EPA. Pundits have blamed Pruitt because of his close ties with the non-renewable source of energy sector and scrutinized his commitment to environmental protection. Under the Wheeler administration the EPA was always looking for deregulation and also reverted several natural approaches from the Obama period.

Public Ecological Strategy Act (NEPA) This is the Trump NEPA organization has revised the guidelines that govern NEPA that require natural effects assessments for major foundations projects. The changes will simplify the assessment process in a way that reduces the amount of ecological appraisals as well as aiding in the process of projects with the approval process.

Preservation as well as Public Terrains The Trump administration was looking for agreements that emphasized extracting assets from open areas. The plan included limiting the size of the public monuments, like for instance, Bears Ears and the Terrific Stairs Escalante in Utah that sparked legal issues. They also opened an asylum called the Cold Public Natural life Asylum within The Frozen North for oil as well as gas penetration.

It's important to be aware of the effectiveness and efficacy of these strategies are subject to debate, with those who advocate that they helped cultivate financial development as well as administrative assistance and apologists expressed concerns over their long-term environmental effects and the United States' global environmental initiative.

4.4 Judicial Appointments and Supreme Court Nominations

In the course of his presidency, Donald Trump made critical legal agreements, such as designations for his High Court of the US. Trump was adamant about moderate adjudicators as well as judges who matched with his legal thinking. This is a brief overview of the legal framework Trump has used and Supreme Court appointments:

Legal Arrangements:

Through his entire administration, Trump made various arrangements with government courts. These included regions courts, court of request and special courts. In naming moderately appointed officials in his administration, he aimed to change the structure of the executive branch of government that had lasting effects. Trump was able to name over 300 adjudicators in various court systems, making an important mark on the executive branch.

High Court Selections:

Donald Trump had the chance of naming three judges to his High Court during his administration. The details of the three judges that he appointed to his High Court selections:

a. Neil Gorsuch:

In the month of January, Trump designated Neil Gorsuch to take over the role that was left after the death of Equity Antonin Scalia. Gorsuch had a modest record as an adjudicator on U.S. Court of Allures for the 10th Circuit. In the wake of Senate confirmation, Gorsuch was confirmed as an adjudicator on the Court of Allures for the 10th Circuit in April 2017.

Partner Equity of the High Court in April of 2017.

b. Brett Kavanaugh:

In July of 2018, Trump designated Brett Kavanaugh as the replacement for Kennedy, who had resigned. Equity Anthony Kennedy. Kavanaugh has served on the U.S. Court of Allures in the D.C. Circuit and was a moderate background. Kavanaugh's choice turned out to very hostile due to allegations of sexual misconduct and triggered a disputeable affirmation procedure. No matter the controversy, Kavanaugh was affirmed by the Senate and was made an official Partner Equity in October 2018.

c. Amy Coney Barrett:

In September 2020, after the death of Equity Ruth Bader Ginsburg Trump named Amy Coney Barrett to fill the vacant position. Barrett was a judge in the U.S.

Court of Allures for the Seventh Circuit and was known for her moderate viewpoints. Barrett's affirmation procedure was speeded up and she was then acquiesced by the Senate within a few days of the final political vote in 2020. The Senate confirmed her as Partner Equity in October 2020. Partner Equity in October 2020.

It is important to be aware of these arrangements as significant as they affected the balance that was the High Court for a moderate greater portion of the time, with six judges inclined to moderate, and three judges inclining towards liberal. The changes in the Court's sythesis could influence the lawful decisions concerning various matters for an extended time to come.

Chapter 5: Post-Presidency And Future Influence

Donald Trump's post-administration actions and the potential impact on the future have been the subject of a lot of speculation and curiosity. After his departure on January 20, 2021 Trump retained his energy on governmental matters and retained areas of strength being in the news.

One of the aspects of his post-administration is the commitment he has made to his friends via various methods of correspondence. Trump has sent his "Workplace for Donald J. Trump" for the public statements he makes as well as employed online platforms for entertainment and platforms, particularly Twitter for sharing his thoughts and ideas. Trump's power to dictate the discussion of his base and to give it to his supporters has enabled him to use his influence and influence public discourse even with no authority from the Trump administration.

In terms of political influence, Trump plays had a significant impact on the formation of what is now known as the Conservative Faction. The kind of populism he has exhibited and his "America First" plan has been heard by a large portion of the conservative base. A lot of conservative newcomers seek Trump's support and come to his policies to reach out to his supporters. Trump's support has been thoroughly searched for, and he's successfully lobbied for newcomers that agree with his plans that has led to some discretionary victories against those rivals.

Additionally, Trump has shown an keen interest in keeping pace with his command of his Conservative Association contraption. He has also advocated for candidates in crucial choices, with the intention of influencing the decision-making of rivals who adhere to the plan he has laid out. The candidate has also negotiated an activity committee (PAC) named "Save America" that raises funds to assist competitors that line to his goals and enhance his political influence.

In spite of his political activities Trump has been looking at different routes to increase his influence. Trump has suggested the possibility of launching his own media platform, to serve as a stage to the people he has allied with and enable the president to bypass traditional media outlets. Although the specifics of such a stage have still to be determined the possibility is that it will provide an instant line of communications with his supporters, and increase the impact of his message.

The future impacts that will be wrought by Donald Trump will rely upon various factors. The level of assistance his base receives, the level of support he gets from his own base, the results of his supporters' the present, as well as the ability to adapt to a changing political environment will play a major role. It's not clear how the Conservative Faction will develop or whether other figures emerge to challenge his dominance within the organization.

It's crucial to know that the public's opinion of Trump is incredibly enthralled. As he continues to inspire his loyal followers however, he also faces massive opposition and criticism. As with all political figures his sluggish impact will be shaped by aspects of the political landscape and the cultural nuances of his happenings, as well as the decision made by him before a long time.

In general his post-administration presidency demonstrated his an impact on his fellow members of the Conservative Alliance and his capacity to influence political discourse. Trump's future impact isn't completely established by how Trump explores the evolving politics and keep up by assisting his followers.

5.1 The Life After the White House: Business Ventures and Media Presence

Following his departure his life, the Trump's is marked with a variety of projects as well as a heightened media coverage. It is important to investigate the activities of Donald Trump following his departure from the Trump administration.

Undertakings:

It is the Trump Association: Trump has focused on his land and the sanctity of his business, which is the Trump Association. Even though it is true that he has given over his daily events to his kids, Eric and Donald Jr. He is still knowledgeable of the essential decisions as well as significant agreements.

Greens and Resorts: Trump is the owner of a crucial array of resorts and fairways all across the globe. He continues to put money into and advancing the properties that have his name on them and are renowned for their lavish amenities.

Permitting and marking: Trump has for quite long time been involved in marking his picture and signature on a variety of items and government agencies. Even in spite of debates about the administration of his predecessor, he's been able to keep up with the authorization arrangements for various Trump-branded items such as clothing, accessories and household products.

Land improvement: Trump has a background with a focus on land improvements as well as his the desire to pursue projects both locally and globally. However the focus of his post-official presidency is primarily focused on overseeing current properties, not developing major ventures.

Media Presence:

Web-based Entertainment: The most popular mode of communication is the internet, specifically Twitter. However it, his admission to important stage for entertainment is restricted because of the restriction he imposed on Twitter, Facebook, and diverse stages as a result of the role his online presence was able to play in the events surrounding the events of January 6, 2021. House of Representatives revolt.

Trump television: Theories have persisted regarding the likelihood of Trump launching his own media company often referred to as "Trump TV." Though no official organization exists at the moment but he has demonstrated an interest in using his popularity and his following to set up an media platform that matches with his political views.

Meetings and appearances in public: Trump has allowed meetings for various news outlets following his resignation. These events have allowed Trump to present his views opinions on a range of topics, which include legislation, strategy as well as his personal history. Additionally, he's been present in rallies, events, as well as gatherings. He has his presence evident in the media.

The Books Trump was the writer of couple of books through his career, such as "The Art of the arrangement" and "Imagine greater possibilities and get your Ass on Business and life." There is the possibility that Trump may continue to write and release books, providing some insight of his life experiences and insights.

It's crucial to know that Trump's post-official activities are contingent on the progress of improvements and may change over time. The media and his activities have been tightly linked, allowing Trump to maintain a large media presence, even after leaving.

5.2 Impact on the Republican Party

Trump's impact upon his impact on the Conservative Association has been significant and broad. Being a lawyer turned financial advisor, Trump brought a novel way of dealing with government as well as a libertarian outlook that resonated with a large segment of the base conservatives. Below are some of the key methods by the way in which Trump hosts had an impact on the crowd:

A Libertarian Shift: Trump's campaign and administration signaled a shift to populism in the Conservative Faction. Trump capitalized on the discontent of many Americans feeling disenfranchised by globalization and its basis of his political party. Trump's focus on movement control trade protectionism, as well as "America First" strategies engaged ordinary citizens, and forged an coalition within the GOP.

The base is energized Trump's unorthodox style of speaking and his unfiltered way of addressing the base of conservatives like any other candidate have before his time. The ability to connect with friends via entertainment on the internet and especially Twitter enabled Trump to bypass traditional media outlets and speak directly with his followers. The enthusiasm generated by the grassroots attracts conservatives and contributes to the increase in turnout for decisions.

Modification of Information: Trump reshaped the Conservative Association's communication on the most important issues of contention. Trump's emphasis on immigration limitation along with line security as well as the protection of exchanges were a break of the conventional conservative position. The president's "America First" plan, which was characterized by an emphasis on domestically-sourced financial interests addressed his core supporters but also sparked a debate within his own party regarding the importance of global commitment and deregulation.

The Party's Devotion and the Essential Problems Trump's reliance in his commitment to the Conservative Alliance was additionally cemented via his influence over crucial decision-making. Trump lobbied and supported young candidates he thought were committed to his policies which often led to victory in these races. Concerns about the possibility of facing crucial challenges from opponents who were Trump-backed pushed many conservative lawmakers to adhere to his plans, increasing his influence within the political party.

Discord and Collusions Moving: Trump's stay in the White House has exposed divisions within of the Conservative Alliance. Some laid-back conservatives are awestruck by his manner and tactics, whereas others took to his methods with enthusiasm. The Trump administration has revealed the dividing lines between traditionalists who are conventional and the emerging libertarian wing that was able to continue working on the subsequent races and is discussed.

High Court Arrangements: Trump's influence extended into the executive branch, specifically with respect to arrangements for his High Court. His appointment and the effective affirmations of three moderate judgesthe judges Neil Gorsuch, Brett Kavanaugh as well as Amy Coney Barrett -- altered the equilibrium of the court and ensured a more moderate portion. These decisions are likely to influence American law for the foreseeable future. They will also be an enormous success for Trump as well as his aides.

Reassessment of Conservative needs: The administration of Donald Trump caused a reconsideration of some long-standing conservatism-related needs. Trump's focus on issues such as immigration, exchange as well as the common financial worries, compelled the conservative party to confront the shifting socioeconomics and preferences of its supporters. It is a constant debate about the direction of the party and its strategy demands continues to shape the current legislative landscape to be conservative.

Although the impact of Trump's presidency to the Conservative Faction is significant however, it's important to be aware that it has a distinct alliance that encompasses diverse viewpoints and aims. The totality of his impact on the party's planned strategies and direction will remain unveiled for a while.

5.3 Legacy and Historical Assessment

Trump's family history and an accurate assessment are topics that continue to be discussed and scrutinized. Similar to any other politician, opinions about his impact and successes vary based on one's perception. In this article, I'll provide an outline of Trump's family history and also the manner the way he's being evaluated by experts in the field of history.

The Trump administration, which ran from 2017 until 2021 was marked by a lack of consensus and division. Allies were often applauded for his eccentric appearance, his outcast personality and efforts to agitate the base of the political system. They also viewed his economic strategies, which included tax reductions and tax liberation, as essential to the work development as well as for the business local zone. Trump's close ally's also appreciated his commitment to moderate characteristics and his selection with moderately appointed officials to the government courts, which includes the three High Supreme Court judges.

One of the most significant achievements of the Trump administration was the tax breaks and occupations section Tax breaks and Occupations Demonstration of 2017 that was designed to stimulate financial development by reducing the cost of corporate expenses as well as providing tax breaks to individuals. Allies argue that this policy contributed to the regions where the pandemic is at its strongest for the economy, including low unemployment rate and gains in financial exchange. Additionally, Trump's administration has facilitated important nonaggression agreements within the Center East, known as the Abraham Accords, normalizing relations between Israel as well as a handful of middle eastern countries.

The media, however, contain a handful of elements from Trump's presidency that they believe that have produced negative results. They claim that his erratic manner of speaking and actions caused political divides in the US. Many commentators are also concerned over Trump's strategy to deal immigration, referring to the shady travel boycotts that focus exclusively on Muslim countries, as well as his organisation's zero-resilience policy, which has led to the division of families along border crossings at the U.S.- Mexico line.

Trump's handling of the Coronavirus disease is another controversial issue. Although his administration accelerated the development of vaccines via Activity Twist Speed, pundits claim that the underlying reasoning behind his dismissing the disease and inconsistent informing hindered the need for a strong reaction and worsened the situation.

The experts in history will likely analyze Trump's presidency within the context of these achievements and disagreements. The long-term effects of his strategies, such as such things as tax breaks as well as liberation, will be evaluated in the light of their economic impact and their viability. The development in the Abraham Accords and their enduring effects on harmony within the Center East will likewise be assessed.

Furthermore, Trump's administration could be examined in relation to its impact on the norms and institutions of American majority rule the government. Trump's ferocious style, his aversion of the media, as well as his disregard for the traditional government integrity raised questions regarding the demise of voting evidence-based rules. The chaos that was engulfed in the U.S. Senate hall, accompanied by a large number of his comrades in January 6th 2021 will be viewed as a sluggish moment during his presidency, showing the ugliness of the divisions that were evident across the nation.

Overall the Trump legacy and a credible assessment is dependent on ongoing debate. Allies praise him for his massive successes in the areas of economy, legal structures as well as the international policy and the media highlight his erratic manner of speaking and handling the pandemic and concerns about the health of his popularity establishments that are founded on his popularity. Finally, time and further examination will provide more thorough knowledge of Trump's presidency as well as its impact to the US.

5.4 Reflections on Donald Trump's Political Journey

Donald Trump's latest political gambit was out and about remarkable, having an lasting impact on American political issues as well as triggering vast discussions and debates. A polarizing figure, his presidency sparked passionate feelings and divided the nation as few other times during the course of time. In light of Trump's political machinations certain key views sound familiar.

The most important thing is that Trump's rise to the driving seat was distinguished because of his ability to take advantage of the discontents and anxieties of a large segment of the American people. Trump's libertarian way of speaking and pledge for "Make America Extraordinary Once more" resonated with many that felt secluded by the globalization process and the politics of the time. Trump's appeal was focused on his image as a scourge as a successful finance executive with the potential to bring his skills in Trump's White House and stir up the political framework.

The investigation of Trump's political incident without acknowledging his unique way of communicating. By making use of Twitter as well as his plain and sometimes disputed statements, Trump skirted customary media channels, and merely spoke to his friends. Although this strategy earned an ardent fan base, it also triggered massive disputes and strained discretionary relationships with local and international performers. Trump's use of online entertainment is a good example of an additional time in his political correspondence in which the distinction between personal and official explanations was revealed to become increasingly obscured.

Trump's strategic plan was distinguished by the combination of modest standards and playful strategies. The Trump administration was in favor of tax cuts as well as a less hawkish approach to matters of exchange as well as international issues. Trump's focus on the future of America first resonated with allies. However, the decisions he made often garnered criticism due to their potential negative outcomes including aggravated pay disparities or damaging international relationships. However, his decisions regarding strategy, like the legal arrangement and the expansion of police force, had lasting impressions on the nation's legal scene.

The Trump administration was also separated by a tense political atmosphere, characterized by constant conflict between the president's office and the different government branches. Reprimands and the confirmation by the Senate also exacerbated the divisions in politics that been present in the past. The Trump time was a time of the challenges managing in an era of heightened partisanship, and was provided a reminder that it is important to keep current with the rules of governance within the framework of popular vote.

In the end, Trump's political gambit displayed the strength of his mystique and his ability to entertain on government issues. His ability to direct consideration and defy the norms of news reporting was unparalleled. In his energetic campaign rallies or unscripted TV foundation, Trump knew how to draw crowds to his events and preserve the most important areas of his strength to be a part of the conversation. Although this strategy has its flaws, and even the critics doubtless attributed it to an important role in his ascendance to the top and forming the political arena.

In the end, a look at Trump's political activities, it is clear that he was an unsettling and out of the ordinary character who has left an indelible impression on American political questions. Trump's administration highlighted the deep divides within the country as well as the challenges of administration at the time with a growing levels of partisanship. Be it you like him or not his impact on American legislation will go getting read and discussed for quite an extended time in the near future.

Chapter 6: Donald Trump A Stem

CLYDE'S HEARTMAN Frazier Jr. belonged to the African-American community in New York. He was the organizer of Harlem Hoops basketball tournament for those living in the city. He was killed in the terror attacks that took place on 9/11. Following his passing, the event must be closed. A businessman who is successful was informed of the incident. He quickly instructed his aides to search for the Mr. Frazier's dad. After they located Clyde's father and the businessman who donated the money to ensure the tournament continued. This businessman was not a different name than Donald John Trump.

The Mr. Trump has a graduate degree from The Wharton School of Finance and is the Entrepreneur of the Award winner for 1998 at the same institution. Trump is the core of a variety of philanthropic and metropolitan groups, including the Board of Directors of Police Athletic League. Trump has been a key figure in the police athletic league. Trump is also the chairman of the highly regarded Donald J. Trump Foundation as well as Co-Chairman of the New York Vietnam Veteran's Memorial Fund. In 2015 the general Joseph Dunford-Chairman Joint Chiefs of Staffwas awarded his Commandant's Leadership award.

Donald John Trump is one the most well-known American television and business personalities who's business interests are real-world the state, sport and entertainment. Even though Trump has made a lot of blunders and is in the main of the time viewed as an ordinary administrator, Trump is remarkable as an enthralling leader.

The Mr. Trump took his first move in his career as a businessman in the office he shared together with Fred. Trump, his father. They were in Sheep head Bay, Brooklyn, New York. Both of them worked for 5 years. "My dad was my first mentor" Trump said. Trump and he contributed in a further way in the form of "I am able to learn a tremendous amount about all aspects of the construction business from his father".

Fred C. Trump was the proud father of Donald. Trump said that, "Some of my best transactions were possible thanks because of my son". In addition "Everything that he touches can change into gold". Following his departure from the office of his father and entering the totally different market of Manhattan Real estate.

Within New York City and around all over the globe In New York City and around the world, there is no doubt that the Trump name is associated with some of the most prestigious of addresses. The famed Fifth

Avenue skyscraper, Trump Tower as well as the luxurious residences, Trump Park, Trump Palace, Trump Plaza, 610 Park Avenue, The Trump World Tower (the tallest structure in the East Side of Manhattan) as well as Trump Park Avenue are just the most prominent.

He. Trump also hold the charge of building his own Jacob Javits Convention Center, famously known in"the" West 34th Street Railroad Yards as well as the complete interior restoration of Grand Central Terminal as part in his plan to transform the nearby Commodore Hotel into the Grand Hyatt Hotel. The development was a further feather on the cap of. Trump when Manhattan's Community Board Five presented him with the honor for "tasteful and innovative reuse of an iconic hotel."

The Plaza hotel, where each bride would like to exchange vows - has been revamped under the direction of Mr.

Trump as praised vociferously by the New York Times Magazine. In addition to this Plaza Hotel, Mr. Trump holds the famous buildings within the house of the Real Estate Building- New Yorkand the St. Moritz Hotel.

The Mr. Trump owns the Nike Town situated located on East 57th Street and adjacent to Tiffany's. The beginning of 2008 saw Gucci, a famous brand from the world, opened their biggest ever outlet anywhere in the world, located in Trump Tower.

The Trump International Hotel & Tower was built in 1997. The 52-story hotel tower is situated at the intersection of Manhattan's West Side, at Columbus Circle It is an amalgamation of super luxury residences and a hotel. The president. Trump hired Philip Johnson as the architect for the layout of the building and the building has seen the most rental and sales rates within the US. This is among the three hotels in the US which received a two-time Forbes Five-Star Rating for the restaurant as well as the hotel. The prestige of the hotel is enhanced after it was awarded the highly coveted distinction that is The Five Star Diamond Award from AAHC. The hotel has been ranked as the most popular Hotel within America. US according to Coned Nast Traveler Magazine. It is a further glimmer in the Trump hotel industry.

The octopus in Donald's business is spreading its tentacles across Chicago, California, Washington D.C, Florida and New Jersey. The octopus spreads its tentacles all the way to Miami and also internationally, within Baku, Azerbaijan.

The late Mr. Trump -"The Developer of the Year" named as such by the Construction Management Association of America and Master Builder recognized by the New

York State Office of Parks, Recreational & Historic Preservation is a prolific author of a variety of books. The autobiography of his father, The Art of the Deal which was ranked first place on the best selling list in the New York Times. Over three million copies the book were sold within a very short period of just four weeks. "The America We deserve" was a masterpiece written by author and author. Trump: The Way to the Top was a quick top bestseller across all lists. A second book by Trump was released under the name Trump The Greatest advice from the real state I've received.

In the course of his successes, He was the owner of the broadcasting rights for three of the most prestigious beauty contests around the globe including the Miss Universe, Miss USA as well as the Miss Teen USA and Miss Teen USA Pageants. Miss Universe Pageant is broadcasted throughout more than 180 nations around the globe. Trump Model Management was founded in 1999, and has since grown into one of the top modeling agencies within New York City.

In the month of January, 2004 the late Mr. Trump had made a alliance together with Mark Burnett Productions and NBC to create "The Apprentice"the reality television showthat broke record for ratings and earned an acclaim. The season premiere was seen by 41.5 million viewers. The show was nominated for three Emmy categories.

In 2005 the year 2005, Trump was in 2005 when. Trump made his hand more dirty by launching a new business, the debut of the Donald J. Trump Signature Collection. It is a collection of tailored clothing and dress shirts, tie as well as accessories such as belts, cufflinks and cufflinks. Trump has also set his name on the furniture market under the name of Trump Home which comprises mattresses, furniture, bedding as well as home décor as well as bathroom accessories. The mattress is the most popular company, Serta.

Chapter 7: A Narrow Escape

In the time that Donald Trump was in his late forties, his assets were awash with debt that exceeded 970 million. The back of his head was up against the wall. Now, he's at 121 on the Forbes Richest people list and owns a net worth of greater than 10 billion dollars. The former president is a prominent Republican Presidential candidate. What helped the writer of the New York Times best seller "The America We Deserve" avoid a bankruptcy? What did he do to turn the trend?

The majority of real estate developers take loans from banks in order to finance their ventures. If they form a strong association with giant money lenders will be more likely to secure the right amount of real land. At the beginning of 1980s, Trump was the focus of the banks and money lenders. They provided $80 million in exchange for Trump wanted 60 million. In the 2015 presidential Announcement speech in 2015, the Commandment Leadership Award winner disclosed that an institution approached the winner and offered him the loan amount of $4 billion. This is how much value there is in Trump's signature. Trump Signature now.

The Mr. Trump expanded his empire by utilizing money loan lenders. He could purchase the Holiday Inn Hotel and Casino in Atlantic City. He constructed two additional casinos in New Jersey including the Trump Taj-Mahal, the largest casino located in Atlantic City- In early 1990s, the demise of Trump Empire started. The economy of the nation was declining. It affected Trump's earning capacity. The president was not able to repay the charges on his outstanding debts. It was time was that Trump was a personal debtor to the tune of $975 million. Marla Maples - his second wife- recounts that one time she was walking alongside Trump when he pointed at the homeless person and told him, "That guy is not enough to earn less than 10 cents, but the guy has an extra $900 million worth of wealth than I do."

Trump was in contact with four key companies in the world of lending money, including Citibank Bankers Trust, Chase Manhattan Bank and Manufacturers Hanover- and as the most likable of people, he managed to convince the four companies to loan him an additional $65 million in order to maintain his business on the right track.

Trump himself said "It was revealed that banks actually liked my work and valued me as well as the things I did."

He then sold Trump Shuttle and later a yacht to Saudi Prince Alwaleed Bin Talal. Trump has also given up control of the

Plaza and quite cleverly transformed his Florida beach home into a hotel. The casinos he operated in Atlantic City were filed for bankruptcy and as a result the interest rates were reduced to pay off the debts of the casinos. The most remarkable trick Trump performed was the conversion of his three casinos in Atlantic City to a single firm under the name of Trump Entertainment Resorts and got $2 billion as the company's first public offering, which resulted in an immense relief for the president as Trump paid off his debts.

He was able to escape from bankruptcy. His name was reinstated on Forbes 400 in 1997. Forbes 400 in 1997 with his net worth at $2 billion. He was not in the ring of Forbes for a period of six year.

Donald J. Trump knows the best time and place to launch the most of. In the 80s, he was a business mogul and was referred to as impertinent man, yet people in the business world knew single characteristic of Trump i.e. that he was competent enough to last. In the decade following, his company was in the midst of going into bankruptcy. With his determination and a dazzling business acumen, He was able to overcome his financial crisis. Today the number one spot is his in the Forbes 400.

Chapter 8: Trump Stoops To Conquer

Trump is a mater in the establishment of his company. He has crafted his brand so that customers are looking to spend their money on purchasing their preferred products from his brand.

Trump has proven to be a huge success for a large part because Trump has discovered how to create a living a rich and successful life Trump leads and lot of people want. He tries to develop his image, and uses his image to explore different business areas and explore areas of opportunity. From the real estate industry to books and clubhouse the new endeavors he pursues have been selected to complement the main picture.

In the event that he wears an outfit in his Donald J. Trump signature gathering or says "You're dismissed" in his wildly popular Apprentice Apprentice the viewers interact. They believe that someone who's millions of dollars, and lost billions more, understands what an appropriate suit looks like just like, the moment they observe him dressing down an opponent when he appears on TV that they are sure he understands the requirements to be an effective director.

One good example of an enterprise that is also using its image to increase the size of the company and discover new revenue streams can be found in Best Buy. Best Buy vanquished the now obsolete Circuit City since it could convince people that it offered the best selection of goods with a higher price and had a more skilled employees. Because Best Buy remains solitary, it's taking the shopper's perception into consideration and using it to improve its private-mark offerings.

Through it's Geek Squad, RocketFish, Insignia, Dynex and Init Brands, Best Buy is putting out esteem-tested gadgets and hardware-related support for people of all ages. This method is believable due to the reality it is the case that Best Buy has invested years making the decision that it understands devices and has a good understanding of esteem. Customers trust Best Buy knows hardware the same way Donald Trump knows extravagance condominiums as well as extravagant outfits.

When dealing with an organisation one must consider what their core competency is prior to moving to new offerings. Wal-Mart tried to make a mistake by attempting to sell equipment under its own private brand, ILO. The customers are confident that Wal-Mart is aware of shabby and Wal-Mart offers the finest assortment of tissues and cotton swabs. The customers don't believe any of the products that claim Wal-Mart is a true expert with devices. In spite of everything, they must buy a high-end television with a screen that is level as well as look for the highest quality at the expense of an dents and scratches segment cost.

Trump's name has been a source of controversy. Trump name has been shown to be strongly associated with the improvement of land in the past, and Trump has put on an impressive display to support the notion that he has properties all over all over the globe. This isn't true However, large percentages of the amazing developments that carry the Trump name don't actually belong to him. After experiencing liquidations, as well as the great and bad seasons of the property market He has found a way to reduce his risk. He has put his name and his face to work, to keep his cost and the cost of introduction to his business to a minimum.

The properties, such as Trump World, in Seoul and Seoul, are able to use his name but haven't been claimed by the owner. There is a fee when he lends his name out and ensures that there is quality control and enjoys the perks of another massive Trump-marked commercial property.

So, he makes up his picture and does not worry about the dangers of not having enough benefits on his financial record. Many officials prefer to manage businesses with massive numbers of people and large resource bases, in order to seem competent. But, as the financial incident has demonstrated companies must concentrate on profits for the sake of value, instead of focusing on impeccable revenue and resource figures. For instance, Lehman Brothers was flush with resources and workers.

Another example of a company who knows how to cut risk and cost while remaining extremely efficient can be found in Body Glove, the creator of sportswear. Body Glove has been making wetsuits since the 1950s, and is now involved in the world of shades, footwear, swimmingwear bags, and a wide variety of products but it's got only a handful of employees. Despite its small dimensions, the company has transformed into a well-known global brand through meticulously affixing its official name to outcomes from various organizations.

Finally, as one of the most effective ways to gain entry into business individuals, Trump is dependably at working. If he's watching Larry King Live, on The Apprentice taking part the festivities of WrestleMania or just strolling along the street, he knows that every second is an opportunity for business and is prepared to take advantage of the possibility. He typically wears his specific ties, and claims that he's at the most recent golf club in a television interview.

He knows that deals and advertisements are all the time and night. Compare that with a star such as Michael Phelps, who neglected to realize the magnitude of his personality had for his capability to get. Phelps was not a snare to his swim career after he was caught with a camera smokin' cannabis nevertheless, he undermined his standing as a person who is likable and has the confidence that you need in the event that you're required to become an uber-star endorser for the likes of Kellogg . The Donald recognizes the value his clever yet unconventional photo is appealing an opportunity, and he makes sure to play the situation up. Additionally, he realizes that viewers watch the show on a regular basis.

Trump is a perfect example of the overabundance that was muddled and sloppy in the last decade Yet, people love his character and are captivated by his character. This is due to the fact that even though Trump is adamant to make massive improvements to buildings to his own name, he requires confidence. He's among the most wealthy men on earth but he is still speaking to a common person. He's not afraid to joke about the hairstyle, his disappointments and all his flaws. This makes him much less likable.

Chapter 9: Business Lessons From Trump- 1986 Entrepreneur Of The Year

Donald Trump knows his gathering of supporters is superior to any the three previous wives. He's focused on it. He doesn't seem to care on the possibility that you love him or don't. There's something in Trump's plain speech "I don't care the things that people consider to be" attitude that appeals to the most ardent Republican people. He is addressing their deepest displeasure and desires against the present leader and the current pioneer of Trump's White House. He's bringing the opportunity for an audience which has been unengaged for at least two Presidential periods.

Similar to Trump's image, your image isn't required to be a part of "everybody." Understanding your target market, interacting and understanding their concerns in a meaningful way is vital.

A Democratic Surveyor Stanley Greenberg, who's distributed vast amounts of research on the typical white laborer's attitudes and attitudes, explains that "there are no greater concern for Trump's supporters than a deterioration of the framework political. They're preparing to shock around the world, and organizations are buying the power, but ordinary people are ostracized." Trump's financial wealth allows his image to be that of an individual who cannot be purchased.

Donald Trump puts on a display of his authenticity legitimate, authentic, and without rehearsal and is a true depiction of who he is. When you hear him express the results you realize that his conclusions are his and not derived that comes from an expert group or polls. He has a reputation which people interact with. Additionally, it allows him to regularly (or maybe not so minor) mistake since he's not subject to the demands by the political elite which is thought to be clean and well-practiced.

Mary Civiello composed as of last night in her Fortune magazine story "What Donald Trump's Outbursts Speak About leadership" and the article's accompanying commentary on his apparent sincerity.

"One explanation for Donald Trump's climb in surveys is because he's real. No matter how many people like his views, a lot of them are pleased that he appears be authentic ... non-scripted, unlike many lawmakers.

The people are seeking authenticity among corporate leaders as well. Children, especially, those that combine their professional and private life on the internet should be aware of how the boss operates outside of the work setting."

Donald Trump was dependably a prominent scholar. He believed in massive arrangements and huge investments in the field of land, seeing the potential. In spite of the fact that Trump did end up in the negative but he was able to achieve a stronger recovery. Thus, he came to become famous throughout the corporate world, and he turned into a television character.

A good leader must constantly plan an impressive the future as well. Like Goethe stated, "Dream without a second thought, as they lack the energy and determination to stir the hearts of people. If you're an entrepreneur who wants to be identified with people's souls and hearts, remember that you must prepare yourself to amaze all the world!

Donald Trump is a man with a lot of energy. He believes it's the vitality that fuels energy and passion is the factor that makes the impossible possible.

The desire to inspire should be the primary goal as a leader. It is essential to be excited about the work you're doing and the direction you're taking. A spirited leader can convey the impression of energy down to his followers and inspires them to continue running an extra mile, stay for an hour more, and fight slightly harder for their cause.

Even though it is true that he was in chapter eleven, Donald Trump has enough self-conviction to be able to in the same position for a second time The place he's in currently is a sign of his determination to bounce another time from disappointment.

It's a common occurrence for people, especially to pioneers. If you're a pioneer, and constantly breaking terrain, the likelihood of crashing is significantly greater than remaining in the same area of experience.

The most important thing to consider isn't how to maintain the distance to avoid disappointment instead, it is how you are able to bounce back in the aftermath of encountering the other. It is the only way to be an innovator and sets you apart from those who remain in their chaos.

Trump has spoken a large number of bizarre things in the war, from provoking statements regarding Mexican colonists to accusing John McCain for not being an "war legend" instead, each latest incident in the media or storm just seems to be supporting his actions in polls. Why is that Trump's core support believes he's telling about his beliefs, regardless of the fact that he's speaking it in a professional elegant manner.

A majority of candidates for political office have their hair so clean and in their appearance that it's almost impossible for their true thoughts and opinions to be expressed. Trump is on the streets all day long, offering unequivocal portrayals of how the way he views it. Trump isn't worried about his image to anyone as it seems.

It's important to not be afraid to stand an entity as an identity, despite the fact that it's disputed. Many companies try to look snobby by attempting to become "standard" and appeal to "everybody." This is important to stand out despite the fact you may lose some customers who do not "get the concept," in the long run, that you keep engaging with the core market of customers who love you most.

Trump does not follow the same model as central gatherings. Every competitor today tries their messages and try to discover the ideal combination of issues and words in order to reach the correct segment of voters. But often, candidates end appearing to sound "center at a." The actual human association with the rival gets involved in trying to appeal to an excessive number of people. Trump appears to be being heard by moderate Republican people because he's inexperienced and unpolished. He's willing to speak in a haze of no planning. It looks like he's talking about whatever's most urgently on the top of his mind right now and there.

This is the case when you purchase your item. It's great to conduct an analysis of the statistics to determine the practicality of a particular item but it's more crucial to be sure that you've got a good thinking. In the event that you're feeling that you feel that way, imagine that the other are feeling the same. I've witnessed a myriad of unique thoughts be diluted and confusing even when there's a large number of cooks at the table. In the event that you endeavor to create your message accessible to everyone and everyone else, you'll wind ending up interacting with no one.

Trump has a lot in common with everyone other presidential candidate we've witnessed in political issues of the past. He seems to have not a feeling of regret or shame. He speaks what he wants to say and he says it as he believes it is, then he continues on and ignores the blamefinders. Did Trump ever apologized to anyone for something? Trump seems to lack the tools to admit his mistakes or for being out of line.

It raises an interesting aspect for your picture When is it appropriate to apologize? If your client has an unfavorable experience with your product is it an appropriate time to express your apology? However, is it advisable to offer an offer of a reduction and move with the rest of your business, explaining it in the form of "Well it's not the ideal customer to our company?" If somebody is upset or confused by an article posted by your business on Twitter If they are, is it recommended to offer an apology? Do you need to ignore the opinions of pundits and try to profit the attention of them?

It's hard to determine what to do when you need to be firm. In the event that you repeatedly apologize it will be the case that you'll offer meals to customers who don't understand the value of the service you provide. In the event you fail to apologize even if you feel that your apology is legitimate, you could damage your reputation. There is a fine line between maintaining your reputation and making the right option. Don't invest the bulk of your energy trying to please clients who are not worth it.

Trump illustrates the value in a certain kind of uncompromising, without-statements of regret method of collaboration. It's almost Zen-like in his stoic refusal to let himself be hindered by matters of importance by being told "too poor." The president simply keeps moving forward and onto the next one. It's a refreshing thing that's about that, and yet there aren't many brands that can do it.

If you're a supporter of Trump or otherwise, it's clear that he's a fascinating standout person on American legislation and business. It's not necessary to end in the mold of Trump to benefit from the way the man has promoted himself or constructed his reputation.

Trump is known to express what is in the top of his list and with clarity. The unfiltered and authentic style of Trump is distinct from the majority of others, which appear to rely on a set of statements and a persona that is recommended. Many users believe it's refreshing. Dallas Mavericks proprietor Mark Cuban shared a wide-ranging assessment of Trump in an interview with Business Insider, "He psyche things that are at the forefront of his head. Trump gives honest answers rather than pre-planned answers."

In general, as people seek honest political leaders, consumers require honesty and transparency from businesses. Do you believe that you're transparent with clients regarding the sources of your food, its management methods, quality as well as estimating? Do you believe that you're prepared to admit when you make mistakes? Are you sure that you're training and educating your employees to speak with clients like persons, rather than following the advice of scripts and strict methods?

Although Trump has spoken to small number of people, he's been a snarky critic of many other people, which includes a significant part of his business associates and his backers. NBC Universal, Macy's, and Serta were among the companies who ceased working with him following Trump's remarks during the presidential crusade's kickoff speech. Univision has withdrawn its participation in its Miss Universe show since Trump has claimed the show, while several associations, such as NASCAR, ESPN, and the PGA had a break from Trump.

Companions who behave improperly or make arguments with statements expose risk to your business in a huge way for the business. Make sure you thoroughly vet your business partners, which includes franchisees, suppliers, organizations, as well as contractual employees like conveyance management providers. Do they have the same qualities as you? Do you have a clear understanding in terms of what's appropriate as well as what lies outside the area of influence? Is it safe to state that you're monitoring their actions on the internet? Are you in a position to make an agreement to swiftly end or alter your association should it become necessary?

It appears that the Republican Party has taken in the most important lesson from Trump concerning the majority of people who are a part of its image. As of the time when I wrote this report there was a debate about Trump hurting or aiding the GOP but it was apparent that people didn't anticipate his machinations. Additionally, the initial efforts to control him or limit the impact of his actions were not successful.

The situation between a political group and rivals is similar to that of the situation with representatives and organizations. It is true that the Republican Party can't control Trump just as you cannot control your representative. Every single employee affects the perception of customers about the image you present. Representatives who fail to adhere to client's needs or strategies or are simply required to perform their own action can cause significant difficulties. Naturally, you are able to remove them from the company, but every now and then you may find that the harm has ended by now.

It is best to make a contract, organize and guide your family members meticulously. Are you willing to sign up gradually? Do you ensure your employees understand and appreciate your strengths? Do you instruct, train and motivate your representatives to become great ambassadors to promote your brand image?

There is not a single bit of this a reference to the underwriting of Trump or as a declaration about my political beliefs. I'm always looking to find what I can learn from different points and sources; Trump has given significant insights from his successes and his mistakes.

Trump has made what remaining in the Republican field seem completely clear. Rand Paul and Ted Cruz were considered by a lot of people to be insurrectionary opponents before Trump made his debut and began to make great assertions. Trump also stole the famed media stage away from Hillary Clinton. Is it safe to conclude that you're making decisions that are making your opponents actions appear unnecessary or even a bit snobby? Instead of merely following trends and trying to bounce off the latest cycle of news do you think you're actually creating the pattern and news?

Chapter 10: Every Nation Needs A Good Foundation

"I'm an builder,"Donald Trump proclaims time and time repeatedly before the throngs of people cheering at his rallies."I construct."

In fact, he's the ultimate builder, literally as well as in other ways. As a literal matter the man has managed numerous prominent construction projects, and has decorated the cities' skylines using his own brand. Additionally, he's established an extremely successful business with the name of The Trump Organization. Many might go as in the direction of calling the company an empire.

"Because I'm a builder I'm well conscious of the necessity to have a strong foundation,"Donald Trump stated once in a self-help motivational recording. "You shouldn't gamble in building, and you shouldn't act reckless and just say, well maybe it will succeed, or maybe not but let's do the idea and figure it out...I must know whether it will be successful or not. Each inch must be considered ..."

"...In the words of getting big ideas starts by doing your homework, and the first step is to be diligent. Do not rely on chance to take you where you want to go, since it will not."

It's a good idea to take a few minutes to let the end of the quote soak in.

A chance event will lead nowhere.

If you leave this book without the wisdom nugget inside your wallet the purchase has made a lot of sense.

Repeat it loudly and with me:

The randomness of life will not get you anywhere.

Good. For those who want to continue using construction metaphors No one wants to build an unattractive red brick home located in Borough, New York. Many dream of becoming high-rises located in Manhattan. The majority of people consider their future, and fantasize about how wonderful it would be as a massive modern, elegant glass tower that is atop the other buildings of others and glowing as the Egyptian night obelisk.

However, here's the problem with Skyscrapers: they're difficult to construct. Extremely difficult. They require a lot of planning and thought. It is necessary to have blueprints and plans and they must be run through a series of sketches before the design is finalized.

Most importantly, Skyscrapers need a solid foundation on which to build.

But when you ask the dreamers of the world about the blueprints or foundation that they plan to use to build themselves into"skyscrapers,"ninety-nine times out of one hundred you will only get a shrug of the shoulders in response.

The body language of the dreamer and general indifference to your query should tell you the truth. answer:"I didn't do effort to work out the way to get there stuff.I simply enjoy thinking about how great it'd be."

It is true that the skyscraper never came into existence by chance. This is also true of those who achieved. All of them had a solid base from on which to build their accomplishments. All of them had a well-thought out plan of action which led to their successes.

The remainder of thischapter will cover the former--the foundation of your "skyscraper"--while the next chapter will get into the nitty-gritty of designing blueprints that carry you to victory.

PassionAnd Ability-The Foundation Of Your Nation

In this article, Donald Trump defines the two important assets that define a person's foundational elements for achievement. These are traits that show aptitude and passion as well as the more straightforward way of putting it:

You should like what you are doing.

Do your best at doing what you are good at.

Passion -Your Fuel For Success

"...This is the most important thing to achieve great achievement. Be passionate. You must be awed by the work you do if you wish to become successful in it. My dad used to tell me this and it's true. It's possible to work seven days per week, but it's not work for me since I enjoy what I do.

If you're not happy with the job you're doing, look for other to be doing, or do it in a part-time capacity until you discover something you love that you love full time. It's impossible to be successful, happy as well as happy or healthy when you're not doing something you are passionate about. It's what it is." Think Big Ten Rules to Success Your Success

My students often have to call out names of the top, most successful and most wealthy person they can dream of from out of the air. When they are bombarded with responses that are thrown out, the name"Bill Gates"is most of the time most popular. This is the perfect illustration of the concept Donald Trump is explaining in the quote.

Think, for a moment you can, the following scenario:

Bill Gates is a fairly typical teenager in the 70's early on. He gets up early then drags himself out of the bed, only to find that you're overwhelmed by the almost all-too-common force of dread that is growing. He is absolutely dreadful of the work that lies ahead.

After an entire half hour of unending procrastination the teen Gates eventually makes it to the garage, and switches at the lamp. In the corner--decorated as if a monolithic gargoyle -- is the expensive and undesirable "present"Billy's father has forced upon the young Gates: a top of the line computer.

As he looks towards the machine Gates rubs his temple before he let out his breath.

"Well...better go back to school and study this dull piece of junk," he groans. "After all, all these dumb computer gadgets are bound make me the most wealthy human on Earth in the near future."

The end of the scene.

Let me know what you think about that scenario. Does it sound like an unlikely scenario for you?

What do you think of Gates' attitude towards computers was what he was saying?

Do you believe it's more probable that Gate up in the early, eager to return to the most recent software creation? The fact that he was obsessed with his laptop throughout the entire day? He pounded away on his computer until late into the morning? Then he had to get dragged away from his keyboard using an encased titanium bar?

We are certain that which one of these portraits is true. We are certain that Microsoft was founded with a teenager's enthusiasm for computers. In the wake of the passion for computers that a billion-dollar company eventually grew.

Trump's story isn't any different.

At a young age, but not yet older than walking, Donald Trump the toddler constructed skyscrapers from blocks under his father's desk. Sometimes, he would go even as far as stealing the blocks of his brother in order to construct his structures more high.

At the age of a child, Donald Trump was extremely agresive. Trump was almost exiled from school due to an dispute with his music teacher over preferences in music, and everything else--changed into a violent assault at Donald's expense.

"As an adolescent, I found myself mostly involved in creating chaos, as for reasons I was able the idea of causing chaos, and I loved to challenge people...It wasn't so much malicious as it was agressive act," he explains in The Art of the Deal.

A determined boundary-pushing swather who has a love of high-rises? The competitive world of New York City real-estate dealing and construction fits Donald Trump like a glove.

As a result it is important to note the issue of the elephant in the room regarding Trump's accomplishments in the field he chose. It's not a secret that regarding his eventual status as a billionaire, one could say that Trump Trump"self-made," it's true that he actually was born to a wealthy family.

It's not a secret that the origins of his massive fortune was aided through a"small loan of one million dollars"from his father.

For some, the massive headstart given to Trump by his father's wealth reduces the importance of Trump's successes in his life. For me, it adds to their value. remarkable.

Being a friend of a couple of so-called"trust-fund baby" friends, I've witnessed personally the lack of a sense of purpose which a lot of people born rich show. To put it plainly, worthless liars. Donald Trump had every reason to be more or less.

Donald Trump has even admitted that his Brother, Freddy Trump, was very similar to the same mold. However, Trump's apparent love for Freddy Trump prevents his from using this negative language.

Instead of being another"trust-fund lying about," Donald used his father's achievements as a way to propel him towards a greater achievement. Success of the seven figure variety.

And Trump did it due to the fact that he was born into the correct family at the appropriate time at the right location, he discovered his passion for the machinations and transactions of the high-profile real estate sector.

Every time and time repeatedly, the tales of those who are extremely successful illustrate this fundamental principle Do what you are passionate about and, most likely, do things you enjoy. Even if it's not one that's traditionally lucrative, like real estate or major cities development You'll do much better off performing it because you're passionate about it. You'll more likely be able to profit from the passion you have because it's something is something you truly enjoy doing.

Perhaps most important the fact that being enthusiastic over something will lead towards...

Ability -Because Passion Alone Doesn't Pay The Bills

"You aren't able to trick individuals, or at least in the short term. It is possible to create excitement, you could do amazing promotions and receive all sorts of attention, and even could even use a bit of exaggeration. However, if you do not give the results, people will eventually get it." The Art of the Deal

The unfortunate truth about love is that, without the capability to support it in a meaningful way, it's an essentially useless value.

It's possible that I'm the most enthusiastic person on earth about Juggling, but if have trouble keeping three balls up in the air, and they don't revolve with a pleasing design, what's the point of my enthusiasm? It's your responsibility to provide what you promise. In whatever you do You must possess relevant skills to can make you useful to others in one manner or other.

The good news is that enthusiasm is a method of making you a better player. The passion I have for juggling will prevent me from quitting after I stumble over the bowling ball for the fifth time. I'll be glued to my book on juggling and will help me commit my entire knowledge of juggling into my brain.

This will spark an enthusiasm for the juggling world as well as lead me to exciting possibilities in the field of juggling.It'll encourage me to search for fellow circus performers who share my enthusiasm for juggling to exchange useful knowledge with other juggling enthusiasts. In the event that I am lucky enough it will lead me to an expert juggling coach who can assist me in the journey of becoming a professional of juggling.

Similar principles apply to business, writing, artistic work, or skilled labor in general. As long as you do not fall into the trap of becoming the kind of person who is a devoted bystander -- someone who is a spectator and gets a sense of second-hand satisfaction out the experience of watching others perform the things they're passionate about. Your desire to be passionate will never stop you from pursuing it to master your trade.

In the event that passion is a catalyst for ability, which happens naturally in things, you will quickly realize that you're able to accomplish whatever you are most passionate about at an official level.

Once you've got the foundation set, the rest of your success will follow.

Chapter 11: Designing Your Blueprint To Success

Time and time it is the case that the theme of this chapter has been the most frequently retread and repeated principle of the self-help category.

There's an excellent reason for this. In the end, it's the most important factor to being successful.

In the broadest sense, that important factor can be described this: set out your goals and then set your sights on making it occur. Don't let your dream go until you've accomplished the results you want.

If you've made a decision about your goals, you need to figure out how and when. But in terms of clarifying the how, you're far ahead of the bulk of humanity.

You see, most people don't set goals. Most likely, at least not in the way they should. There are occasions when the time for making New Year's Resolutions comes around, but even at times, only half-hearted commitment. In the majority of cases it is the case that most people simply drag their feet and latch on to any favorable events that happen to them.

The thought process of a drifter sounds like this:"What's the matter with a job open at the local auto factory? I've never thought of becoming factory workers, however the advantages are nice and I've no other work to do and so, why wouldn't I?"

It's true that we need drifters to fill those gaps and to keep the economy moving. There's nothing negative or embarrassing about drifters. Everyone needs a huge pool of people who are drifters in order to sustain its own.

However, that doesn't mean that you need to be either. There's always a lot of applicants lining up to get the perfect job opportunity with amazing advantages. The job market will never be empty. way too many people who are drifters. In addition, there will always be too few who have a clear goal in their lives with the commitment, determination as well as the proper"blueprint"to follow through.

Instead of drifting instead, become a builder just as Donald Trump. Make a list of what you'd like and start to develop the plan of how you will achieve it. Everybody is capable of both of these things, but however, very few do.

The Three P's-Your Blueprint For A Blueprint

One simple method I prefer to implement for goal setting and achievement is what Motivational Speaker Tony Robbins calls the The Three P's.

Purpose

Plan

Policies

You're Purpose will be the final result you want to achieve. You're pursuing what you want to achieve in your the world. The more precise and specific the goal you set more specific, the greater.

Your goal is written to stone right from the beginning and will not be altered until you've reached it. Your foundation is the foundation of your life. It's your primary plan to achieve your success. It's impossible to move forward in the world without taking the direction you want to go in.

It's impossible to make it through an adventure without making a map of its route. This is just common sense, however, it hints at the vast majority of people to some bizarre reason. People sit and wonder,"Man! What is it that makes my life awful?"

If you ask them two inquiries in their response:

1. "Well I'm curious, where did have in mind in five years' time?

2. "What did you do to stand out of the way of getting that to happen?"

The initial question would make them a mess. In reality, they were unsure of where they would like to be just five years ago. Therefore, "nowhere" is exactly what they got to.

Don't get that is stranded at sea with no clearly defined destination in your your mind. Instead, map your route and dedicate yourself to your journey to the fullest extent of your ability.

The second "P," but it is flexible than the final goal. The Plan you have created is the one that will be used to achieve the goal that you've defined. While it is important not to alter your plans in each direction in which the winds are blowing but you should acknowledge that occasionally an excellent plan fails. Sometimes a plan can take longer than anticipated, or unexpected events can occur within our plans and must be addressed in a timely manner.

In the event that you've set your sights on the goal of your non-changing goal You can become more flexible in the strategies you employ to achieve that goal. Donald Trump is famous for his open-ended approach to business.

"I don't get focused on one deal, or even one approach," he discusses in the book "The art of the Deal." For reasons of course, I've got many balls out of the way, since the majority of deals fail regardless of how attractive they appear at first.

Once I've signed a contract, I'll always have at least half a dozen strategies to make it happen, since everything can go wrong, even with the best laid strategies."

It's still important to establish a strategy to achieve your goal prior to time and execute it with the expectation that it's going to be successful. The most successful people believe in themselves and their goals or else they'd give up and leave whenever they saw difficulties.

The third 'P' is your policies in order to reach your objective. The purpose of a policy can be explained in a few words. These are measures that have been put in for the purpose of ensuring the success of. If, for instance, you notice that your partying habits are hindering your capacity to reach the goals you have set, you can adopt a policy that restricts going out on weekends to drink while you work towards your goal.

Utilize your foresight and apprehension to look ahead and pinpoint possible faults that could be within your strategy. Make sure you follow the right policies in order to prevent them.

One kind of policy you could implement to increase your opportunities is the practice of "value engineering" your time. In this article, Donald Trump explains value engineering's value on construction sites within The Art of the Deal:

"One technique we used to cut costs was by using the concept of value engineering. Consider, for instance, that the architect you choose to work with shows the door you'd like to install that has four hinges.

When you are ready to approve the door, have an engineer examine it then say, 'Wow at it, you'll only require two hinges on the door over, or three in the event that you wish to complete an excellent job.'So you remove one hinge costing ten dollars. Then you multiplie that by 22,000 doors. And the savings on this tiny piece amounts to about $20,000."

The same way that Trump took a look at the particulars of his workplaces to cut costs and save money, you should look at the specifics of your routines and routines to cut down on time that can be put in achieving your goals. Take away, for instance, those second breaks in the morning that you're not using every morning, and over time you'll be adding hours that aren't being counted toward the ultimate target.

Chapter 12: Wheeling And Dealing Like Donald Trump

The work we've done is impressive within a couple of short chapters. We've laid a solid foundation for the nation, and learnt how to sketch out their personal plan for success, in black and white.

In this chapter, we'll get into the brass tacks Trump-tricks-of-the-trade to help you along on your journey of nation building.

There is the common thread between them that is individuals. Even in this constantly technologically dependent world, the vast majority of transactions are performed by humans. The flow of money flows through humans.

Everyone from all different walks of life remain the gatekeepers of all for reaching your goals. Be able to handle individuals effectively and you'll be successful in everything you are involved in.

Know Your Audience And Always Speak Their Language

A man who has an education worth a million dollars from one of the top business schools around the globe, Donald Trump sure talks quite like a typical person. In the manner he talks and how he uses his words one would believe you were hearing a blue collar employee if you heard any of Donald Trump's rallies that he has made up in the absence of any previous knowledge of the person.

Donald Trump has endured great critiques from his political adversaries because of this style of speech. Many have suggested that he speaks as a simpleton. I'm sure they're fine with Trump since in a huge way"simpletons" are exactly the kind of people Trump wants to communicate with in the campaign.

Donald Trump knows that winning over an entire group of ivy college students by delivering eloquent talks will not put Trump into the Whitehouse. In the end, he'll need the blue collar vote, which is a more diverse group of America.

The most savvy Trumpologists can all affirm that Trump has been adapting his image to appeal to an audience since he put his hat into the arena of the presidential election in 2016. Take a look at an interview with a older Donald Trump in the 80's--or maybe an episode from the early seasons of The Apprentice and you'll notice a more balanced man who has a more sophisticated style of speaking.

It's not a secret: Trump has always been the ultimate showman The incredibly sluggish appearance he's been displaying lately is part of a strategic political plan. Trump knows who his audience is and has modified his rhetoric to attract the people they are.

There is great benefit to making the same. If you're seeking a fair price on a car's maintenance work, it's not a good idea to get in touch with the mechanic in the same manner as you might with a college teacher.

A lot of people oppose this kind of disguise, believing it to be fraudulent or disreputable. If that's what you think you're that's great. Do not compromise your moral values to be successful in your life when your ethics are more important for you than the achievement. However, if you've got an enlightened ethical code, that's worth considering.

If You Don't Like The Discussion, Change The Conversation

"The second thing I conduct when speaking with journalists is to keep it honest. I do my best not to mislead reporters or appear defensive as these are the most common ways people end up in difficulties with the media. If a reporter confronts me with a challenging inquiry, I make sure to give a positive response even if it requires changing the subject.

In this case, for example, if somebody wanted to know what negative impact this world's highest building could be having to the West Side, I turn around and discuss what New Yorkers are entitled to the highest building in the world and what boost it would bring the city to be able to claim this honor once more.

When reporters ask me why I build only for the wealthy and wealthy, I explain that rich people aren't the only ones to benefit from my buildings...I add that the buildings such as Trump Tower have sparked New York's revival." --The Art of the Deal

What Donald is referring to as "framing an affirmative answer," some may also refer to it as "spin," or the art of "spin." He's doing something a bit contradictory in his quote when he starts in the context of saying the way he speaks to reporters "straight" but this isn't really the point he's making with this particular quote.

It's one of the most fundamental concepts that is in the minds of those involved in PR and political matters: if you do not enjoy the topic do not answer it. Instead, use it as a springboard to pull the discussion in a slightly different--more favorable--direction.

It is not necessary to have an audio device across your face in order to take advantage of this vital technique to build a nation. Do you have a boss who is snarky about your work? You can deflect the criticism to protect your position. Do you need to have a confrontation with your coworkers? Avoid it to save your valuable time or energy.

It's nice if were able to be "straight" with all people we come across and go through our lives without a hitch. And most of the time, you could. However, sometimes the environment will require a little subterfuge for your survival and a successful career. This is a normal thing that goes from the fact that you have to look to your best interests.

Instinct - Learn To Listen To Your Gut
Donald Trump was once--briefly--invested in a start-up oil venture that by all common sense and analysis seemed to be a no-lose proposition. Yet, as his investment was getting close to being finalized, Trump awoke one morning in a

state of discontent concerning the transaction.

"One morning, I got up and something did not feel right," he says in his book The art of the Deal. "I got in touch with my friend and said: Listen I have something which bothers me.

Perhaps it's because oil is in the underground and I'm unable to find it, or perhaps it's because there's nothing innovative in the idea. However, in any event I'm not sure that I wish to venture in. Then he said, "Okay, Donny, it's your decision, but you're wasting a fantastic chance."

"The rest of history is history, naturally," Trump concludes. "Oil went total hell for a while afterwards, when the business the group purchased went into bankruptcy the investors he invested in made a loss on every dollar they placed in."

The instincts you have are there because of a reason. Follow your instincts.

Instincts are a thing Donald Trump would say you are either born with or don't have. I'm not sure. I think that all of us possess instincts. All we need is to be aware of how we can listen to them.

The Midwest is located in the heart of America's storm alley, Mother Nature makes people be aware of their intuition regularly. Each year, an event occurs that isn't like the other.

Despite the fact that by all appearances this appears to be typical of a storm, an underlying feeling of anxiety creeps up your stomach that you cannot get rid of. Sure enough, tornadoes have arrived in the midst of those feelings and wrecking everything that is that is in their way.

Find out more about the causes that tornadoes and other natural catastrophes such as meteorological ones result in. With regard to the extent of property damage they cause, the quantity of people killed by them is shockingly small.

This is a result of the technological infrastructure that we have in our society as well as the fact that humans have evolved an extremely sophisticated and evolutionary sense of this sort of issue.

This instinct doesn't just apply to natural catastrophes. People have instincts as well as our decisions, just similar to what Donald made with his oil investments. Problem is that the majority of people with time learn to not trust their intuitions.

www.ingramcontent.com/pod-product-compliance
Lightning Source LLC
Chambersburg PA
CBHW071441080526
44587CB00014B/1937